W9-BTQ-261

SARATOGA

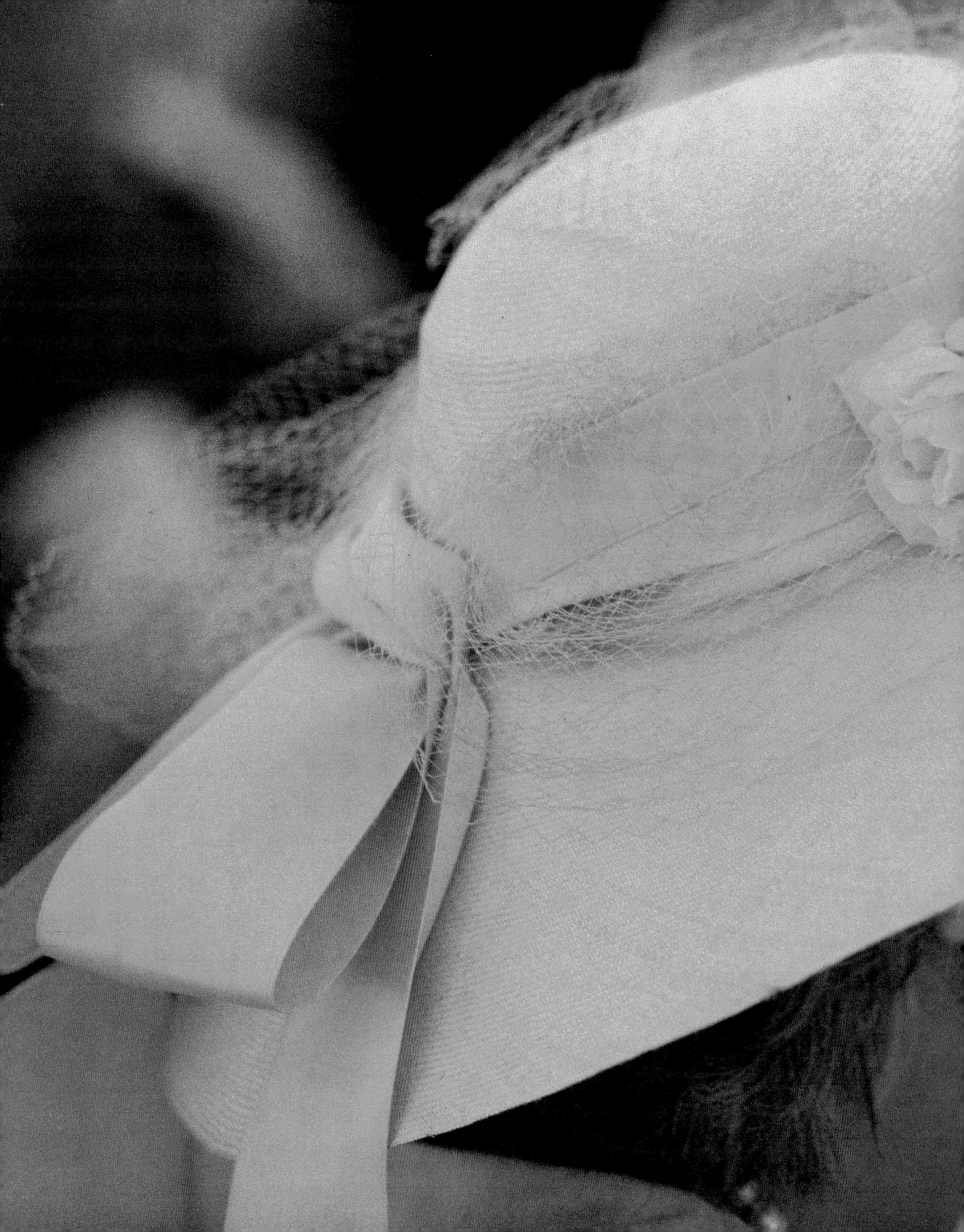

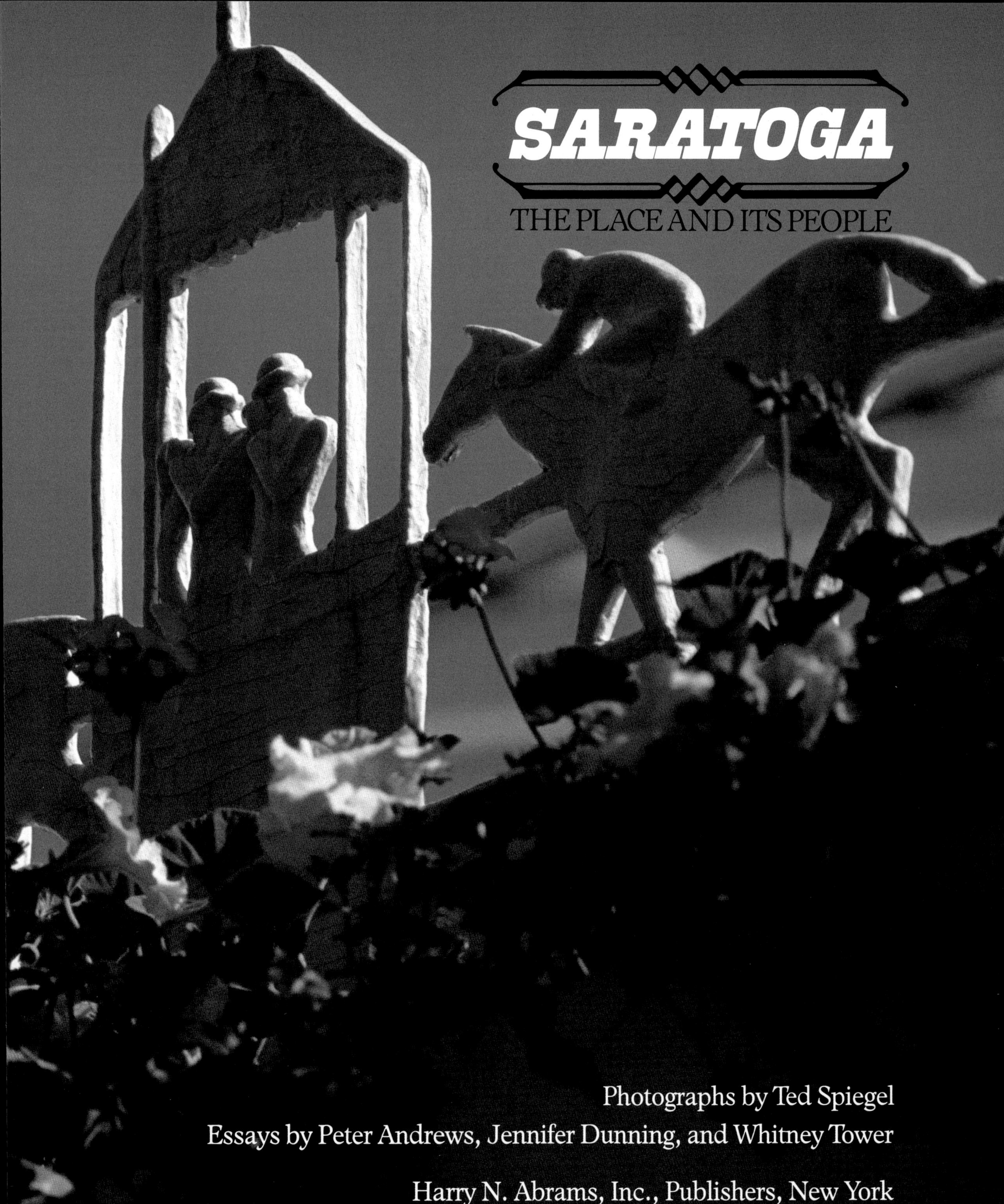

SARATOGA

THE PLACE AND ITS PEOPLE

Photographs by Ted Spiegel

Essays by Peter Andrews, Jennifer Dunning, and Whitney Tower

Harry N. Abrams, Inc., Publishers, New York

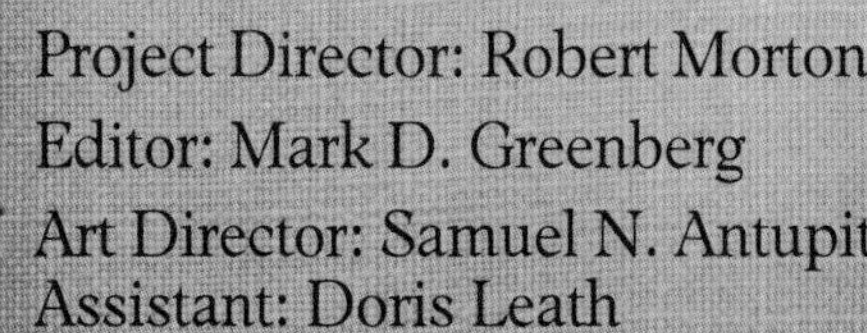

Project Director: Robert Morton

Editor: Mark D. Greenberg

Art Director: Samuel N. Antupit
Assistant: Doris Leath

PRECEDING PAGES
Fantasy never seems far from fulfillment in Saratoga, be it a workout on a misty morning on the main track, a walk through the Saratoga Battlefield, a spin by the dancing waters of Congress Park, or enchantment in the pirouetting presence of the New York City Ballet at the Saratoga Performing Arts Center, a stately invitation to dwell in Clinton Street's Victorian world or an opulent welcome into a North Broadway sitting room, the timeless poise of a Saratoga lady or the perpetual promise of a fortune-filled day at the nation's oldest track; time is never simply here and now.

THIS PAGE AND OPPOSITE
No small wonder that Victorian visitors—and modern antique seekers—set out conversation piece spoons, bearing witness that they had seen and been seen at Saratoga during its centuries-long summer season.

Library of Congress Cataloging-in-Publication Data

Spiegel, Ted, 1932–
Saratoga, the place and its people.

Contents: 1. History/by Peter Andrews—
2. Arts and architecture/by Jennifer Dunning—
3. Racing and the social life/by Whitney Tower.
1. Saratoga Springs (N.Y.)—History.
2. Saratoga Springs (N.Y.)—Description—Views.
3. Saratoga Springs (N.Y.)—Social life and customs.
4. Architecture—New York (State)—Saratoga Springs. I. Andrews, Peter. II. Dunning, Jennifer. III. Tower, Whitney. IV. Title.
F129.S3A53 1988 974.7'48 87-24131
ISBN 0-8109-1518-9

Published in 1988 by Harry N. Abrams, Incorporated, New York.

A Times Mirror Company

Printed and bound in Japan

CONTENTS

PETER STUYVESANT
NEW YORK
SARATOGA

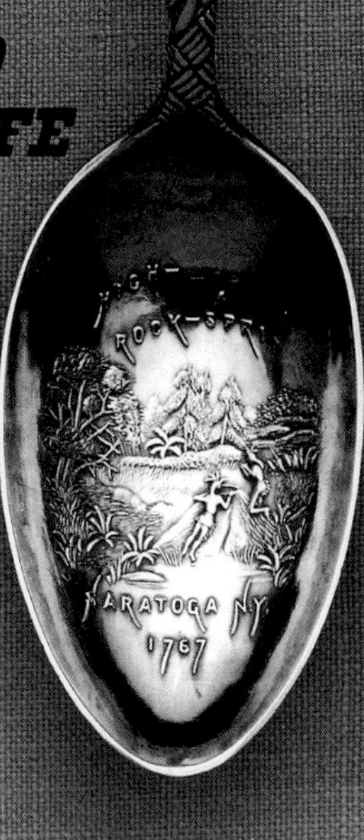

SARATOGA N.Y.
1767

NEW YORK
HIGH ROCK SPRING SARATOGA
1767

BOTTLED BY THE
STATE OF NEW YORK
SARATOGA
GEYSER
GENUINE MINERAL WATER
NATURAL-SPARKLING-ALKALINE
BOTTLED AT THE
SARATOGA SPA
HATHOR

Prologue

THE SPRINGS

Saratoga

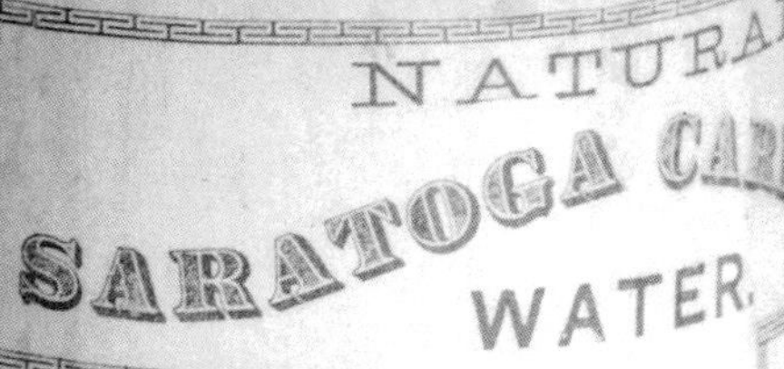
NATURAL
SARATOGA CARLS
WATER.
SPOUTING SPRING.
PROPERTIES.
"CONTAINS MORE CARBON-IC ACID GAS, LITHIA AND ALKALINE PROPERTIES THAN ANY OTHER WATER AT SARATOGA. INVALUA-BLE FOR DYSPEPSIA, KID-NEY, LIVER AND STOMACH DISEASES, ACIDITY OF THE STOMACH, NERVOUSNESS, HEADACHE AND ALL DIS-ORDERS OF THE BLOOD.
TAKEN AFTER ALCOHOL-IC EXCESSES IT TONES UP THE STOMACH AND CLEARS THE HEAD.
SARATOGA CARLSBAD SPRING CO.,

CARLSBAD SPRING
TRADE MARK

5 till. 6 A.M
6 ... 7 P.M

"The first taste of the waters
is not always lovely."

From *Saratoga Illustrated: The Visitor's Guide to Saratoga Springs,* 1882

"Life Sketches" at Saratoga's Congress Spring appeared in Frank Leslie's Illustrated Newspaper *of August 27, 1859, which remarked: "What a crowd is here. Fashion and folly, age and youth, beauty and ugliness, virtue and vice, honesty and hypocrisy."*

During the nineteenth century, members of the leisure classes who were looking for glamour, a cure, or simply a little rest and relaxation frequently "took the waters" at luxurious spas in Europe or America. This often meant literally taking a plunge into malodorous sulfur baths or guzzling quantities of spring water "vitalized" by carbon-dioxide gas. Medicine declared these foul-tasting and foul-smelling waters a cure for many, if not all, diseases, and although it is unlikely that these waters ever really cured anything more serious than a case of galloping dyspepsia, those who took them harbored a faith in their curative powers sufficient to make them at least mildly restorative. The waters themselves, of course, were only a short, sour moment in a regime of sweet pleasure. The best spas offered sumptuous accommodations, splendid vistas, good music, excellent wines, and kitchens guaranteed to make the poor sufferers forget the aches and pains that had driven them there in the first place. In an era of gluttonous excess, spas offered the unbeatable combination of unmitigated indulgence and spring-fed expiation.

In America, Saratoga was the first and remained always the preeminent spa. Located in a narrow valley near the southern foothills of the Adirondacks, it lay in the territory of the Iroquois, and for centuries the waters of the Medicine Springs of the Great Spirit had been revered by the Iroquois as a gift from the god Manitou, who had stirred and thus vitalized them.

While geologists now believe something more complicated than a

THIS PAGE
Empire Spring's pavilion and bottling house
OPPOSITE ABOVE
Excelsior Spring and part of Excelsior Park
OPPOSITE BELOW
The air-tight barrels or "reservoirs" into which Excelsior Spring water was pumped

divine stirring once took place in that valley, they are by no means agreed on how the mineral waters of Saratoga Springs in fact came to be. Some believe the mineralization of the waters derives from salt deposited by a primeval sea that once covered much of New York state. Others attribute it to a now-extinct volcano. Still others ascribe it to chemical reactions taking place far beneath the earth's surface. But if the source of the mineralized waters is uncertain, their passage to the surface has been well documented: A long geologic fault is present in the rock beneath the surface of the valley, and it is along this fault and its lateral branches that just about all the known springs of Saratoga exist.

Of these springs the best known is High Rock Spring—the Iroquois's Medicine Springs of the Great Spirit—a cone-shaped rock about six feet high from a mouth at the top of which salty water once bubbled forth and then receded to a level just below the mouth. It was to this spring that the Iroquois in 1771 brought Sir William Johnson, the British superintendent of Indian affairs in North America and a great friend to the tribes of the Iroquois Six Nations. Sick with recurrent dysentery and a severe wound, Johnson received drafts and baths of the medicinal waters and, after four days, had recovered sufficiently to return to his home in Schenectady. Johnson immediately spread the word of his astonishing cure, and the spa at Saratoga received its first testimonial.

Saratoga grew slowly, but by the middle of the nineteenth century, it had become a boomtown whose official raison d'être may have been its

springs, but whose real draw was the racing, the cuisine, and the glittering display of fashion that made Saratoga a byword for ostentatious high living. By the 1880s, guidebooks to Saratoga listed at least twenty-five springs—some spouting like the famous High Rock and Geyser springs, others lying in wells like the Congress and Union springs—each of whose waters were painstakingly chemically analyzed and prescribed for the cure of specific ills. Indeed, the otherwise languid routine of a Saratoga day always included a brisk walk, usually in the morning, to one of the springs, there to imbibe the miraculous waters whose appearance was described in an early guidebook:

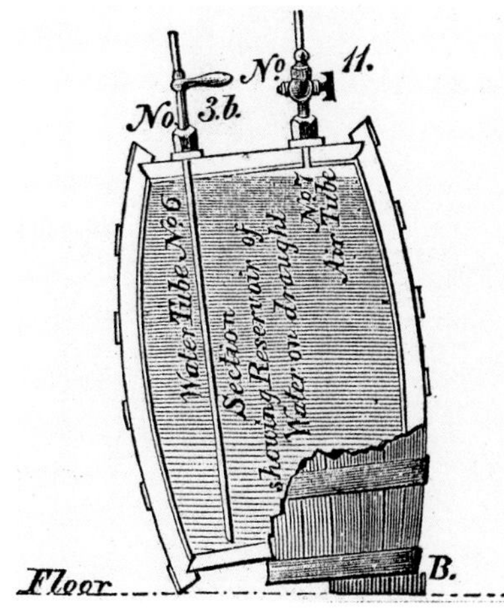

> When first dipped from the wells, the water is limpid and pearly, and full of bubbles. That from the spouting wells gushes forth in creamy whiteness, and resembles soda-water in color and action. The gas quickly escapes, and the still water has a wonderful purity.

The author of this guide admitted that the first taste of these wonderfully pure waters was "not always lovely," but "after the first blush, the water becomes exceedingly enjoyable..."—so enjoyable, in fact, that he warned against a too-free indulgence in their "pungent, acidulous and salty mixture." The author then went on to list the numerous diseases whose cure might be effected by the spring waters. Summing up their medicinal effects, he said:

> They increase the force of the heart and arteries, promote digestion, favor the action of the nutrient vessels, increase the peristaltic movement of the bowels, cleanse the system through the granular organs, and impart strength and vigor.

Nineteenth-century medicine placed great store by "cleansing" the body of impurities—bleeding, for example, was still much practiced in surgery—and mineral waters served that purpose quickly and with practically no ill effects. The habits of the leisure classes in this era of conspicuous and excessive consumption made one curative aspect of these waters especially important:

> Perhaps there is no class of mineral water drinkers who enjoy a visit to Saratoga so much, or who realize so fully and so speedily the benefits arising from drinking the water, as the class of persons known as "free-livers." They suffer from functional disturbances arising from too much food. But when daily drinking the water they are wholly exempt from all inconvenience arising from such surfeit not only, but can use double the quantity of food and drinks previously taken, and experience no inconvenience....All such of the above class as have become more or less diseased from liberal living, may have their stomachs restored to a healthy condition by the use of this water.

The waters couldn't refill your purse if you bet on the wrong horse, but apparently they could redeem your stomach from an ill-advised menu!

Saratoga's fortunes rose to their height in the prosperous decades that followed the Civil War. During those years, it vied with Newport as the place to be when the "seasons" ended in New York, Paris, and London. Those who went in for hyperexclusivity still stopped at Newport, but those who liked a somewhat more democratic good time went to Saratoga. Ladies, and gentlemen, too, showed off fabulous wardrobes, ate sumptuous meals, lost fortunes at the gaming tables and the track, and each morning piously refreshed their bodies at the springs. Great hotels rose up, as did wildly eclectic cottages, and bizarre entertainers competed for attention with more respectable show people. But as the Gilded Age came to a bumpy close with the outbreak of hostilities in 1914, Saratoga, too, seemed to be hearing the last strains of its long waltz.

Congress Water, taken at its source in the Congress Park Pavilion, was no stranger to a nation that believed in the curative powers of mineral waters. Ever since 1823, when Dr. John Clarke began bottling the Congress Spring's alkaline offerings, liquid health had been shipped from summer's pathways into winter's parlors.

Many years before the social cachet of Saratoga faltered, however, the springs themselves had looked to be in danger of exhaustion. In the 1880s, methods had been devised to extract from the waters carbonic acid, which was used in carbonating bottled beverages. Owners permitted drilling and pumping at a rate that would soon diminish if not totally exhaust the springs.

The inhabitants of Saratoga watched this exploitation of their life-giving resource with trepidation, finally appealing to the state government at Albany for rescue. In 1909, the state agreed to purchase most of the functioning springs and much of the wooded area surrounding them for a state reservation. By then, however, the waters were severely depleted—indeed, the two most famous springs, High Rock and Congress, were permanently exhausted—and almost ten years were needed before most of them could function as they once did.

Dr. Simon Baruch, a native of Austria who had earned his medical degree in the United States and had served as a surgeon with the Confederate Army, was especially interested in hydrotherapy, and he saw in Saratoga the potential for recreating in America the sort of elegant spa he remembered from Europe. His son, Bernard, the famous financier and advisor to presidents, inherited his father's fascination with hydrotherapy and his hopes for the rebirth of Saratoga.

In 1929, the younger Baruch encouraged Franklin Roosevelt, then governor of New York, to appoint a commission to plan the revitalization of Saratoga; the legislature was likewise persuaded to appropriate funds to finance the project; and residents of Saratoga themselves offered to contribute. In 1935, the new Saratoga was opened to the public, and it was surely a rival to the Baden-Badens of the Old World. As George Waller described it in *Saratoga: Saga of an Impious Era:*

> The area in which the mineral springs burst from the ground after long years of filtering through subsurface layers of rocks had been converted into a great park with gently rolling lawns and glades through which curved Geyser Brook. Huge shade trees bordered the promenades and carefully graded

walks, elms, birches, particularly pines with their scent perfuming the air, and eleven miles of bridle paths threaded through the groves.

The springs were housed in three pavilions designed in a mixture of Georgian and Williamsburg Colonial. The brick-and-limestone Hall of Springs, in which marble fountains spouted waters from the Geyser, Coesa, and Hathorn springs, was graced by silver and crystal chandeliers; an orchestra played from a balcony; and those who had taken the waters could stroll through lounges and arcades until the waters took their effect: in all, a grand monument to man's unquenchable thirst for quick and painless remedies.

By the 1930s, medical science was looking with some doubt on the medicinal effects of bathing in or drinking mineral water, and so the state hedged its promotion of Saratoga, emphasizing the "rest and relaxation" offered by the waters and the pleasures of the resort rather than any specific curative effect. Still, the pavilions were equipped as if they were indeed medical institutions, and they offered, as George Waller noted, "mineral water baths, massage, heat and light therapy and similar services in private and semi-private rooms" in addition to quantities of spring water just for drinking.

This second incarnation of Saratoga was not destined to last long. Crowds came to take the waters in their new settings, and the bettors came in August to play the horses. But the sobriety of the Depression years and the restraints of wartime dampened the exuberance that had always charac-

terized a Saratoga summer. After the war, the automobile helped speed people to Saratoga, but it also took them away just as fast, and business suffered.

OPPOSITE ABOVE
The Saratoga Vichy Spouting Spring
OPPOSITE BELOW
High Rock Spring
THIS PAGE
The Red Spring

Medical science, too, seemed to be speeding past the old town. If in the 1930s it had looked skeptically at mineral-water cures, in the 1950s it positively disdained so organic a regime; miracle drugs were replacing miraculous waters. And so, despite the temples erected to its honor and the adroit promotion of its healing properties, Saratoga's water gradually lost its power to lure the multitudes. The horses continued to run in August, drawing the same high spenders, but except for that one month, Saratoga was little visited, and her pavilions became quaint, faded reminders of a more splendid—if more gullible—era.

But Saratogians themselves never ceased to believe that there was something in that narrow valley that could soothe the body and the spirit, and by the 1960s, the town seemed once again reborn, having added a month of music to the traditional month of racing and a performing arts center to the grounds of the springs. The crowds came back.

Now they come to sit in the open air and watch ballet dancers and listen to musicians, and of course, to watch the horses run. But surely they come, too, to get just a glimpse of what it must have been like once to be fed, pampered, admired, and cured while bands played and geysers spouted. And "high-livers" can still take the waters!

CONTINENTAL HOTEL.
SARATOGA SPRINGS, N. Y.
GARDEN PARTY
PROGRAMME.

Chapter I

HISTORY

by Peter Andrews

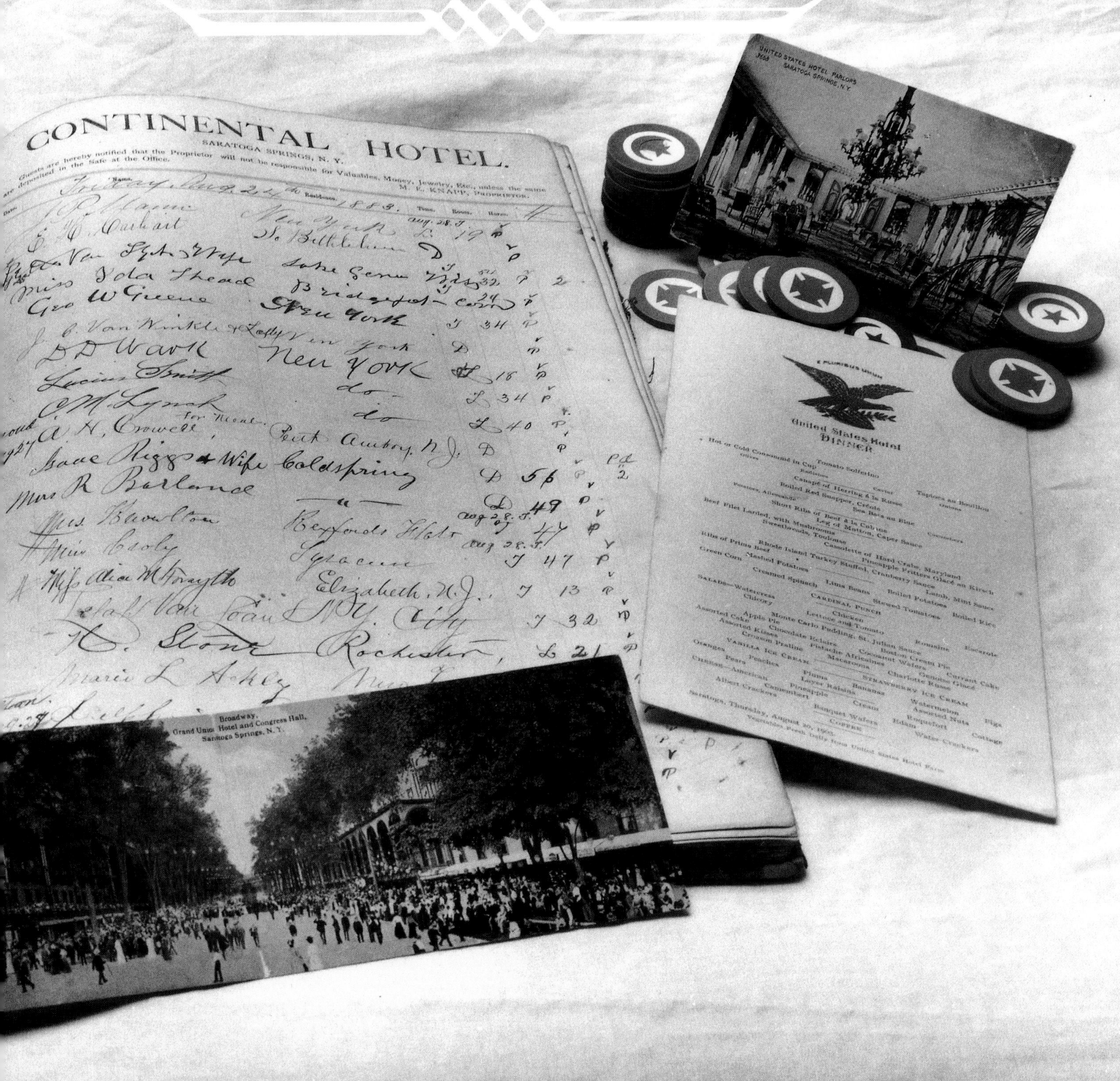

"... this village place I fear will prepare more souls for destruction than those efficacious waters will ever heal infirm bodies."

Mrs. Dwight, *Personal Diary,* 1826

During the latter part of the nineteenth century, when it seemed that many Americans had absolutely nothing to worry about, Saratoga Springs was where they went to get away from it all. Mark Twain came to shoot a little pool and John L. Sullivan came to try his hand, with considerable lack of success, at the gaming tables. John Drew, known as "The First Gentleman of the American Theater," acted out Shakespeare on the lawns to amuse his moneyed friends sitting on the veranda. Lillie Langtry, queen of the stage and mistress of the king of England, caused a minor scandal when she appeared one afternoon wearing shoes with bright red heels. For more than a century, Saratoga never lacked for celebrities who filled the sporting pages and theatrical gossip columns of the day. But the true stars of Saratoga were the freshly minted merchant princes of America going about the difficult and demanding business of being rich. And what a glorious show they put on! The turn of the century was a time of opulent ostentation, and Saratoga stood as the undisputed international center of extravagance.

"Not the Prater of Vienna nor the Unter den Linden of Berlin, not even the Champs Elysées of Paris," wrote one enthusiastic visitor, "offer a more dazzling display of fashion, beauty and wealth."

Diamond Jim Brady, who started out as a bellhop and became a millionaire selling railroad equipment, was never one to understate anything. He put it succinctly for much of American society. "Hell, I've got the money," he allowed. "It's time I had some fun." Brady came to Saratoga to show off the kind of haberdashery $12 million could buy. In most places, the sort of

PRECEDING PAGES
With more than 11,000 hotel beds and a legion of private accommodations in 1882, Victorian Saratoga Springs could host a goodly cross-section of pleasure seekers.

OPPOSITE
"Taking the Waters at Saratoga," a front-cover subject for Harper's Weekly—A Journal of Civilization, *records 1890s fashion: wasp waists for ladies and double-breasted vests for men.*

man who had the buttons on his underwear fashioned out of precious stones could expect to make something of a splash, but at Saratoga Brady was just another pouter pigeon among visiting dandies for whom forty changes of clothes was just enough to get them through the day. In one brilliant season a Western Union clerk wooed and won the hand of Florence Vanderbilt, the wealthiest heiress in America. Leonard Jerome, who was to become the grandfather of Winston Churchill, came to race his horses, and John "Bet-a-Million" Gates came to gamble.

Gates was a dynamic plunger who had made his first million at the age of twenty by turning downtown San Antonio into a giant cattle pen to demonstrate that his new product, barbed wire, would work. Gates was a good judge of fast horseflesh, and once he did so well at the track that he had to send a man with a market basket to fetch his winnings and bring them back to the hotel.

Together, these brash industrialists with their sheaves of crisp, new bank notes forged the spirit of Saratoga; beautiful to behold, lots of fun, loaded with money, and according to the old aristocracy that was being shouldered aside by its exuberance, more than a little vulgar.

The resort scene at watering holes such as Saratoga and Newport was something wonderfully new and gaudy in American life and vastly appreciated by those who could afford it and even by those who could not. Again, it was Brady who summed up the expansive attitude of the times. Stuffed with lobster and his arm around an ample Lillian Russell one evening as they watched a fireworks display illuminate the night sky, Brady sighed and wondered aloud, "Oh, God, Nell! Ain't it grand?"

Although some historians have traced the Saratoga springs back to 500 B.C., their discovery is generally credited to Iroquois Indians some time in the late fourteenth century; they called them the Medicine Springs of the Great Spirit. The Iroquois, who had a legend for every occasion, said the water had come from the Great Spirit in answer to the prayers of a dying chieftain.

The first European known to avail himself of the healing properties of the waters was Sir William Johnson. In 1771, the English Superintendent of Indian Affairs in North America was suffering from a catalogue of ailments, including a musket ball in his thigh from the French and Indian War. According to Saratoga legend, an infirm Johnson had to be carried on a litter to the springs, but after four days of drinking and washing himself in the salty water that bubbled to the surface, he was so rejuvenated that he was able to walk back much of the way to Schenectady under his own power.

A word on the nature of mineral springs may be in order here. Springs are created by water that, after collecting minerals from the earth as it flows in deep, underground streams, is forced to the surface by natural gasses. Since earliest times, such springs were believed to contain healing properties. To believers, the waters have been mixed by that master chemist, Nature. When drunk, they were, and still are, variously thought to act as an aid to digestion, a laxative, or as a cathartic. When used for bathing, mineral springs were the

An 1820s view of High Rock Spring gives no hint of the summertime metropolis that will host health-and-happiness seekers in another 50 years. The first "cure house" rests atop the hill, harbinger of a score of hotels that will welcome summer celebrants by the Gay Nineties.

original Jacuzzi, bringing relief to tired muscles. Skeptics maintain any "cures" effected by mineral springs can be attributed to the relaxed atmosphere there, which allows the body to heal itself. Regardless of reservations concerning the medical efficacy of mineral springs, it is certain they are pleasant and do no harm.

In any event, it is likely that Saratoga Springs would have become a popular New York summer spot even if it had been forced to ship bottled mineral water in from Albany by stagecoach. Located in the southeastern foothills of the Adirondack Mountains, Saratoga is blessed with warm summer days and crisp, cool evenings. The area has been a resort since the Mohawks first left their villages for the summer to live in simple shelters made from tree bark on the bluffs overlooking the lake country. What is now Saratoga Lake was so still and quiet that the local Indians considered it sacred to the gods and felt that anyone who was canoeing on its surface and spoke a single word would be immediately swallowed up and never seen again.

By the late eighteenth century, the springs had gained a measure of fame, but the available accommodations were somewhat short on what has since become known as "ambience." A New England traveler, Elkanah Watson, wrote grumpily to a friend, "I met with a dozen respectable people sojourning at a wretched tavern. The wildness of the region and the excessively bad accommodations made me recur to the condition of Bath

When Gideon Putnam pioneered Saratoga Springs' hospitality, he proclaimed his kinship to General Israel Putnam of Revolutionary War fame by the most direct means: a graphic recounting of "Old Put," bare-handed, throttling a wolf in its den during the winter of 1742. Was the implication that one could sleep safely with a Putnam on guard?

(England) in the barbarous ages when, several centuries before Christ, as the legend says, the springs were discovered by their salutary effect upon a herd of distempered swine wallowing in the mud."

Where there is a natural resource in America, however, builders and entrepreneurs are never very far behind. In 1811, the Saratoga of cheap boarding houses and dank tavern rooms began to give way to more comfortable accommodations when Gideon Putnam, of the distinguished Revolutionary War family, began work on the area's first decent hotel—a much grander place than the three-story frame hotel he had erected some ten years previously. The resort town of Saratoga Springs was beginning to take shape. In 1818, the community saw its first billiard table and listened to its first dance orchestra.

There is no municipal statue in Saratoga to the memory of Dr. John Clarke, but there should be, for it was this canny Yorkshireman who made Saratoga internationally famous. Called "Doctor" Clarke only as a courtesy, he had amassed a large fortune operating one of the first soda fountains in America, where he had learned something of the popularity of carbonated beverages. Clarke had come to town in 1823, and the master merchandiser could not resist dabbling in the opportunities offered by the town's natural springs. Preceding Coca Cola by a century, Dr. Clarke took a simple, basic beverage, Congress spring water, and bottled it. This was during the start of the great patent-medicine craze in America, when various curatives were frequently nothing more than syrup laced with alcohol or narcotics. But here was an "all natural" panacea. Saratoga water was generally perceived as a cure for everything from tired blood to dropsy. The waters may never have actually cured anything, but they were free of foreign substances and almost certainly better for the consumer than gin. In short order, bottled Saratoga water became a staple in genteel American homes. More important, people came from all over the country to drink the sparkling water from a special pavilion that the doctor had fitted out with Doric columns to resemble a Greek temple.

The creation of a health spa in Saratoga was perfectly suited to the spirit of the times. The European gentry had been availing themselves of mineral baths without a social qualm since the Middle Ages, but as social historian Mary Cable has pointed out, to the average nineteenth-century American male, still burdened with the vestiges of a Puritan conscience, "leisure was a suspect thing. He stayed at his everlasting grind because he was afraid of being criticized if caught with his hands folded. When the first resorts came into being, therefore, they called themselves health spas, for if one were sick one might be excused for not working."

The first "patients" started arriving in the early part of the nineteenth century and quickly grew into a Niagara of people seeking to restore themselves.

Officially, Saratoga was known as "The Queen of the Spas" to distance it from such lesser summer institutions as Cape May, New Jersey. But, with the kind of elliptic conversational shorthand so frequently favored by insiders, regular visitors took to calling Saratoga simply, "the Springs." If you

A nineteenth-century paperweight encapsulated a legend: Iroquois Indians partaking of the curative waters of High Rock. The political sachems of modern Saratoga Springs honored this depiction of discovery by making it the city seal.

had asked which springs were "the Springs," you probably didn't belong there in the first place.

As social arbiters are constantly reminding us, the line separating elegance from ostentation is tissue-paper thin. Saratoga stepped over that line almost immediately. As a newly affluent America enjoyed the fruits of economic expansion in the early nineteenth century, the streets and dining rooms of Saratoga became a kind of social exhibition hall where fashion-conscious women could strut their stuff.

Washington Irving watched with a particularly jaundiced eye as ladies poured into Saratoga every summer from all parts of the country to compare wardrobes. It was a contest, Irving wrote, "that awakens a spirit of noble emulation between the eastern, middle and southern states, and every lady hereupon finding herself charged in a manner with the whole weight of her country's dignity and style, dresses and dashes and sparkles without mercy at her competitors from other parts of the Union. The lady of a southern planter will lay out the whole annual produce of a rice plantation in silver and gold muslins, lace veils and new liveries; carry a hogshead of tobacco on her head and trail a bale of sea island cotton at her heels while a lady of Boston or Salem will wrap herself up in the net proceeds of a cargo of whale oil, and tie on her hat with a quintal of codfish."

In the beginning, life at Saratoga was somewhat placid. Guests were generally content with a morning visit to the springs where they drank mineral-spring water from long-stemmed cups handed to them by liveried attendants and then dinner back at their hotel at two o'clock. A promenade around the veranda and out on the street to show off the wardrobe for the day took up

As the Civil War ended in 1865, Mr. Smith of Pennsylvania, Mr. Jones of New York, and Mr. Garcia of Cuba hastened by steamboat to Albany and connecting railcar to the Union Hotel at "The Springs." Their dome-topped baggage, soon to be known as Saratoga trunks, bore finery for a season of social jockeying.

the rest of the afternoon. This, followed by a light supper and perhaps a small musicale in the evening, was considered sufficient excitement for one day.

All of that changed dramatically on July 3, 1833, with the arrival of the Fire Fly, an English-built locomotive pulling along the first luxury railroad train Saratoga had ever seen. Until the development of rail travel, a few wealthy visitors to Saratoga came up the Hudson River to Albany by steamship, but most made their way laboriously by overland stage. With the arrival of the railroad, however, the Saratoga boom was on. In a single year, the number of visitors to Saratoga jumped from six to eight thousand.

A railroad train cannot slip quietly into town the way a horse-drawn carriage can. As a result, Saratoga turned a bit raucous. George Waller, the most energetic chronicler of the scene, whose history, *Saratoga: Saga of an Impious Era*, puts every subsequent author in his debt, described the scene nicely:

"The arrival of each train was signalled by a bell clanging in the depot cupola, and in a matter of minutes, the barnlike station was a scene of cheerful bedlam. Natives hurried to catch a glimpse of the notables and fashionables among the newcomers, and visitors hastened to greet friends and acquaintances. Porters lined up on the platforms and as the train whistled and screeched to a halt began shouting the merits of the hotels they represented. Outside, omnibus and hack drivers took up the cry, and the spirited horses waiting with landaus, dogcarts, phaetons and barouches stamped their feet impatiently."

Whether the intended stay at Saratoga was for a week or a month, just packing for a trip to the spa was an enormous chore, and the need for hoop-skirted ball gowns—Saratoggery, they were called—was so great that a special, flexible, high-domed piece of luggage known as a "Saratoga trunk" was devised just to hold enough of them to get a socially ambitious lady through the season. *Leslie's Weekly*, a popular women's magazine of the time, referred to them as "open mouthed monsters of summer campaigns waiting for the gems of summer attire to be buried within them."

During Saratoga's long reign as America's most notable resort, the city gave its name to all manner of social artifacts that have become woven into our language. As is generally well known, the ubiquitous potato chip was first created in Saratoga: A diner at Moon's Lake House once complained that his French fried potatoes were too thick, and the chef, in angry hauteur, sliced them paper thin and dropped them in hot fat, thus creating the "Saratoga chip." Waiters vied to have the finest serviette presentation at their tables, and one unknown napery artist created an intricate shape of a flower basket with the ends turned up, which is still called the "Saratoga fold." Ladies adopted what became known as "the Saratoga walk," considered particularly useful in catching the passing male eye: the shoulders were held back while the stomach was tucked in and the chin raised high and then, declared one practitioner, "walk, wiggling head, limbs, body and especially the bustle."

There is no better place to show off a new dress than at a dance, and refined musical entertainments soon gave way to a series of grand balls where guests shamelessly danced the polka, a dance considered so risqué that Queen Victoria had banished it from court functions.

The American penny press was always on the lookout for a bit of social scandal to spice up its pages, and no one had a keener eye for such things than James Gordon Bennett, publisher of the New York *Herald*. Bennett was something of a social scandal himself; he once was bodily thrown out of the home of his then fiancée when he arrived drunk for a New Year's morning levee and absentmindedly relieved himself in the fireplace. But that never stopped him from passing vigorous comment on the morals of others.

The so-called fashionable circles of Saratoga, Bennett thundered, "are wholly destitute of cultivated taste, polished manners, or moral feelings sufficient to check the introduction of foreign licentiousness and corrupt morals."

The indecency of the polka, Bennett told his astonished readers, "stands out in bold relief from anything we have ever witnessed among the refined and cultivated *ton* of European cities. It even outstrips the most disgraceful exhibitions of the lowest haunts of London and Paris."

To be able to get to the equivalent of a low Parisian haunt for the price of a railroad ticket to upstate New York was a bargain few could resist, and Saratoga soon became not only a crowded boomtown for the newly rich but also for those who just wanted to be around to watch—and perhaps pick up a little money of their own.

Not everyone was pleased with the moneyed egalitarianism of Saratoga. All decent people used to be acquainted with each other, and if they were not, one gentleman could always tell another simply by knowing his address. But now, anyone with the price of a hotel room took himself to be as

The charms of a summer spent far from America's teeming metropoles were recounted to Harper's Weekly *readers in the clearest of terms: "Witness a ball at the Congress Hotel—the gilded saloons—the softened lights—the delighted revelers—the happy group of juveniles—the tired infant, half-startled from its dream of pleasure by fairy music—the tender mother gazing with mingled anxiety and satisfaction at her gay young family—the fond father bending over the group he loves so well."*

good as anybody else. Old-line New York patriarchs, who had carefully avoided the company of anyone but their own kind during the business year, often found themselves vacationing in the company of persons who would never have been invited to their homes.

"Hundreds, who in their own towns could not find admittance into the circles of fashionable society," noted one patron, "come to Saratoga where they may be seated at the same table with the first families of the country."

The mingling of so many social classes at Saratoga caused a certain amount of domestic unease, and book publishers rushed a series of helpful works into print on resort etiquette for the unwashed, which reminded them that finger bowls were not to be used for rinsing out the mouth or spitting into. It was also considered bad form to ask a newly made resort acquaintance what he did for a living lest the occupation prove unsettling. A stockbroker could not honestly expect to be comfortable in the company of a sausage maker.

A glittering resort where the seeking of pleasure was all but social requirement, Saratoga was largely insulated from the mundane cares of the rest of America. Intermittent cycles of economic recession or even panic did not concern Saratoga. Times were never so bad that there weren't enough rich people to fill the hotels. Even the Civil War did not intrude deeply upon the life at Saratoga. But like many parts of the country fortunate enough to be far removed from the fighting, it prospered as a result of the conflict. It mattered little whether people were weary of being in the war or simply tired of profiting from it, Saratoga seemed a particularly pleasant place to come and be amused.

Almost from the beginning, the forces of virtue and the seekers of pleasure had been struggling for control of Saratoga. Dr. Billy Clark, a vigorous evangelist preacher, had come to Moreau in Saratoga County and established America's first temperance society there in 1808. At first, these abstemious tourists were welcome. However, it is a fact of economic life that pleasure seekers are bigger spenders than believers in temperance. And although the city fathers were as virtuous as any public officials of the time, under the social pressure of a wartime morality, they permitted Saratoga to give itself almost entirely to the immediate enjoyment of this world in preference to the rigors of pursuing the glories of the next.

The wedge was gambling. It had always been understood that gentlemen, among themselves and within the discretion afforded by a private room, could risk money on the turn of a card. But now professional gambling was to be permitted in Saratoga.

The most prominent champion of the new order was a magnificent roughneck named John Morrissey. Born in Ireland, Morrissey came to America when he was a young boy and grew up as a street-gang fighter in Troy, New York. Never formally educated, Morrissey was nineteen years old before he could read his own arrest record, which included burglary, assault and battery, and attempted murder. Always good with his hands, Morrissey became a professional boxer and was briefly the American heavyweight champion after whipping the great John Heenan in eleven brisk rounds in 1853. After that, "Old Smoke"—who had won his nickname when he

BOBBETT-HOOPER SC

THIS PAGE
In 1859, on the eve of the Civil War, the music-filled gardens of the Union Hotel proved a fine retreat from the bustle and heat of America's growing cities.
OPPOSITE
Ten years later, battle-tested blue-bloods of the New York National Guard's Seventh Regiment reunited beneath swaying Chinese lanterns in those very same gardens—to recount days of glory on earlier reconnaissance missions.

knocked over a stove while beating up a rival for the affections of a New York City madame—went into politics, after a fashion, by serving as an enforcer for New York Democratic party machine bosses at Tammany Hall. For these services, he had been favored with an interest in a number of gambling establishments in the city, and in 1861 he moved to Saratoga with a supply of roulette wheels, faro boxes, and playing cards to open up a summer business.

John may have been something of a tough customer, but his proud boast that "no man can say that I ever turned a dishonest card or struck a foul blow" and his raffish spirit sorted well with sporting citizenry of Saratoga. Although he never gained the social respectability he had hoped for, he made a considerable fortune, which must have been some solace. Morrissey's great creation was the Club House, a gaming casino for the rich of such conviviality that when Coal Oil Johnny Steele lost ten thousand dollars at cards one evening he nonchalantly put another ten thousand dollars on the table to buy drinks for the house. He'd come back. Club House patrons always came back because, although the losses suffered were sometimes staggering, Morrissey's reputation for honesty was never called into question. Commodore Cornelius Vanderbilt, generally considered to be the richest man in America at the time and one who did not treat his own reputation for probity lightly, was a regular patron at the Club House and well known as a friend of Old Smoke. The Commodore's public approval of Morrissey was recommendation enough for anyone.

Morrissey's most lasting contribution to Saratoga was the introduction

From high fashion on Broadway to "High Life Below Stairs," the summertime world of Saratoga Springs piqued the curiosity of a nation that had not yet created Hollywood. The readers of Harper's Weekly *noted that Chinese lanterns and patterned parasols adorned Saratoga's promenades, that bustles and French coiffure were everywhere in evidence, that postbellum prosperity brought fancy dress, fine cigars, and photo albums into the lives of even the supporting cast at Saratoga.*

Families enjoying the pastoral view from a thousand-foot-long piazza were sheltered by one of American civilization's greatest wonders—the Grand Union Hotel. By 1871, Warren and Charles Leland could host 1,400 guests at their sumptuously served dining tables. With 737 rooms awaiting their summertime guests, they offered an experience in hotel living matched only by the grand hotels at European spas.

of horse racing. He built the first track in 1863 and then cast about to start a racing season. The timing could hardly have been worse. With the Civil War grinding into its third year, the Union Army had stripped the countryside of horses that could barely walk let alone run at a decent pace, but Morrissey was well connected in racing circles, and his friends William Travers, John Hunter, and Leonard Jerome formed a racing association and managed to come up with twenty-six horses, enough for a four-day race program beginning on August 3. A horse named Lizzie W. romped home over a three-mile course to become the first winner in Saratoga racing history. The meeting was such a huge success it became too big even for Morrissey to handle. The association moved to a larger and more impressive layout the following year and began a new season by introducing the Travers Stakes, still one of the premier events on the national racing calendar. In short order, Saratoga was seeing crowds as large as ten thousand a day come for the racing. Between races, the local sports devised their own betting game known as Fly-Lo. Each bettor dipped a lump of sugar into honey, and the owner of the cube that attracted the first fly collared the money. If that were not amusement enough, a few fortunate gentlemen could get up a syndicate by peering into the unshaded windows of Lillian Russell's boudoir and bet on how long it would take the voluptuous star to struggle into her corset before heading off for dinner.

By the end of the Civil War, there was so much loose money lying around Saratoga that even the most expansive spendthrift could hardly find ways to spend it all. Alexander Stewart had parlayed a small linen-importing business into a $40 million fortune from the proceeds of what was to become Wanamaker's, the largest department store in the world at the time. Stewart came to Saratoga and promptly became the largest hotelier in the world. He bought the old Union Hotel for some $500,000 and put a like sum into refurbishing it. Not unreasonably, he renamed his establishment the Grand Union Hotel. Its specifications made it sound more like a public-works project than a hotel. Situated on seven acres with each of its two wings stretching out for a quarter of a mile, the Grand Union could accommodate some one thousand four hundred guests in almost nine hundred rooms along two miles of hotel corridor. The establishment required an acre of marble and twelve acres of carpeting. Stewart, as they say in current advertising usage, "spared no expense" in making his hotel the most modern of its day. Passengers were whisked to their floors aboard the latest Otis elevator, and less than a year after Thomas Edison invented the incandescent lamp, the Grand Union was wired for electric light.

Technological marvels, like the electric arc light, bedazzled Saratoga visitors.

Although there were a few private mansions in the area, the social life at Saratoga centered around the grand hotels with their self-contained glories. *Leslie's Weekly* called them "perfect villages." Saratoga was always considered gauche when compared to Newport, its great rival as a summer resort. The American novelist Henry James, who trembled like an aspen leaf at the thought of anything vulgar, had been to both resorts and found the European splendor of Newport with its private cottages and its rigid class consciousness more to his liking than the gaudy hotel life at Saratoga, where all men with enough greenbacks were considered equal.

"After Saratoga," he wrote, "Newport seems really substantial and civilized. Aesthetically speaking, you may remain at Newport with a fairly good conscience; at Saratoga you linger under passionate protest. At Newport, life is public if you will; at Saratoga it is absolutely common."

This was something of a minority view. Most social commentators of the time preferred Saratoga's gaudy bustle to Newport's comparatively restrained elegance as being more in keeping with the American ideal. As *Harper's Weekly* said, "Saratoga reflects our national traits to a degree not true of Newport. The latter has an air of aristocratic exclusion and leisure far less lively than that engendered by the commingling of classes at Saratoga. Beyond any other American resort, Saratoga is a social microcosm."

If Saratoga was a microcosm of American society near the end of the nineteenth century, then it is small wonder that much of European aristocracy looked upon the United States as a land of wealthy, undignified parvenues. Johnny Steele always preceded his arrival with a full minstrel band playing in blackface. Peter Lorrillard, the enormously wealthy tobacco heir, cut such a rough-hewn figure in Saratoga society that the society reporter for the *Police Gazette* suggested he adopt as his coat of arms "a cuspidor couchant, with two cigars and a plug of tobacco rampant."

The closest Saratoga ever came to seeing understated elegance during this period was Evander Wall, when he came to dinner wearing a full-dress coat from which his English tailor had, by accident or design, snipped off the

SUMMER COTTAGES OF THE GRAND UNION HOTEL.

STAIRCASE AND VERTICAL RAILWAY.

DINING HALL.

CIGARS CIGARS

BERGHAUS DEL.

GRAND UNION

Mr. Otis's pneumatic elevator, or "vertical railway," delighted guests at the Grand Union Hotel. A three-story, cast-iron balcony, 800 feet long, unified a facility that had continually expanded at the site first utilized by Gideon Putnam. When diners looked for friends in the 200-foot-long dining hall, they had to have good distance vision!

THIS PAGE
By 1874, the magnificent new United States Hotel had hoisted its banner, and visitors rushed to sample its hospitality. Spurred by the competition, Alexander T. Stewart, the new owner of the Grand Union Hotel, expanded and remodeled to retain his claim as "the biggest and the best."
OPPOSITE
At a Grand Union Garden Party in 1879, guests waltzed briskly past the sketch artist of Frank Leslie's Illustrated Newspaper, *whose readers were told, "There is but one Saratoga. It is unique. It is special. It glitters, sparkles, flashes. It reigns absolutely."*

tails. Even in the easy-going social atmosphere of Saratoga, this was rather too much, and it was not until Wall showed up in the same outfit at a dinner party in the far less important New York resort of Tuxedo Park that the garment was accepted as proper attire for a gentleman to wear to dinner.

One day in 1890, Joseph Smith, the head usher at the United States Hotel, noted in his diary that the season was "especially replete with wealthy and conspicuous visitors. All the millionaires of the land seem to be in Saratoga."

During that period in America known as the Gay Nineties, no place in the land was quite so gay as Saratoga. This was the heyday of Diamond Jim Brady. There was nothing retiring about the super salesman of railroad equipment. One biographer estimated that Jim's personal jewelry, which went to such striking items as a set of diamond studs in the shape of locomotives, was worth about $2 million. What Jim didn't wear, he gave to his assorted mistresses and to his much-beloved Lillian Russell. For her amusement, Jim gave Lillian a bicycle with her initials in diamonds and emeralds on the handlebars. Even her little Japanese spaniel, "Mooksie," was not left wanting. Jim gave the dog a gold-and-diamond collar valued at close to two thousand dollars. Jim was always giving away something. Although he never smoked himself, Jim handed out fifty-cent cigars as if they were calling cards. Brady's traveling cigar supply was so large that one of his Japanese houseboys managed to steal enough Havanas to open up his own cigar store in New York.

THIS PAGE
Victor Herbert composed many of his operettas while summering at the Grand Union Hotel.
OPPOSITE
"In one corner of the piazza of the United States Hotel a knot of lynx-eyed gentlemen daily congregate. They seat themselves on rude wooden chairs, speak in that low tone dramatists relegate to conspirators; ever and anon consult telegraphic slips or pocket memoranda, whiffing the while cigars that would have made the mouth of that arch scamp, the ex-Khedive, water from envy. This Eldorado is known as 'Vanderbilt's corner,' and in the center of the railroad magnates sits their monarch, Mr. William H. Vanderbilt, a word from whose lips makes or mars millions."
Frank Leslie's Illustrated Newspaper, *August 30, 1879*

The atmosphere at Saratoga had become more elegant when the mantle of the community's leading gambler passed from "Old Smoke" Morrissey to Richard Canfield. Canfield had known a few brushes with the law before coming to Saratoga. He honed much of his refined image by embarking on an assiduous self-improvement program of reading cultural books taken from the library of a Rhode Island prison while serving a stretch for illegal gambling. Eventually, he developed such a keen eye for fine art that he was accepted into the prestigious Walpole Society as a fellow connoisseur and had his portrait painted by his friend, Whistler. Even when his fame as a casino owner had spread to such international proportions that he was known as "The King of Gamblers," Canfield, whenever required to state his profession, always said simply, "gentleman." His refined bearing was such that he got away with it.

Canfield had made a small fortune running an establishment in New York City that specialized in giving patrons of the nearby Delmonico's restaurant a bit of sport to go with their dinners. Rich from the proceeds of his New York place, Canfield bought the old Club House following the death of John Morrissey and, after fitting it out with crystal and marble and imported Scotch carpeting, reopened it as the Casino. Now Saratoga had a facility fit for its glittering clientele.

Following the European example, Canfield insisted on evening clothes, and his customers, always delighted to do anything European, gladly complied. This raised a delicate problem. Canfield knew from experience that few things could ruin the line of a gentleman's dress suit as carrying either a

THIS PAGE
Celebrities flocked to Saratoga: most prominent among them were Diamond Jim Brady and, on his arm, Lillian Russell, queen of the American music hall.
OPPOSITE
Famed politicians like Horatio Seymour, twice Democratic governor of New York and loser of the 1868 presidential race to Ulysses Grant, came to Saratoga for the 1876 New York State Democratic Convention. His political fox hunt after Boss Tweed of Tammany Hall eventually led to Tweed's downfall.

revolver or a large wallet. Since gambling at the Casino required lots of money—chips were sold in denominations of up to $100,000—Canfield instituted lines of credit for his favored customers. They needed it. William Collins Whitney once dropped $385,000 at the gaming tables while waiting for his wife to dress for dinner.

Canfield installed a famous French chef, Jean Columbin, in his kitchen with orders to set the finest table in America. Columbin must have done so, for several of the Casino's regular customers remarked that it was well worth losing the odd thousand dollars just to sample the master's way with pheasant. The Casino restaurant lost perhaps as much as $75,000 a year, but Canfield, wallowing in profits of the gaming tables, was glad to underwrite the cost.

Money can be a powerful magnet, and Saratoga became a celebrated cultural center as international performers, drawn by the high fees offered by places such as the Casino, came to town. Enrico Caruso sang opera at Convention Hall, John Philip Sousa played marches, and Victor Herbert, America's most beloved composer and conductor at the time, played whatever he wanted to at the Grand Union. Herbert, who always arrived with his own personal orchestra of sixty players, commanded the biggest fees, but as modern day stars at Las Vegas have discovered, Herbert found it was but a short walk from the podium to the roulette wheel. The affable Irishman left as much cash on the table as he took in at the box office. Like most plungers who came

"WHEREBY HANGS A TAIL"
A CUT AND DRIED TAIL BY TILDEN.
BUT NO HEAD.
SOME BODY WANTED
NOTICE THIS WILL GROW INTO A HEAD
DORSHEIMER FOR LIEUT. GOV. N.Y.
THE END IN SIGHT
THE GREAT EXTREMITY OF THE TICKET
HEAD'S THEY LOST
TAIL'S THEY LOST.
REFORM IS NECESSARY IN FOX HUNTING.
UNFOLD A TALE ABOUT THAT
REWARD TO THOSE THAT CAN FIND THE FOX
HE DID A TAIL UNFOLD
THE HAT TRICK
IS IT A SWALLOW TAIL?
TWEED COULD A TALE UNFOLD.
REFORM IS NECESSARY IN TRICKS
THE DEMOCRATS HAVE DROPPED SOME-THING
HOW TO FILL THE VACANCY IS THE QUESTION.
SCIENTIFIC RESEARCH
ANOTHER EXPEDITION (BY THE N.Y. HERALD) IN SEARCH OF THE FOX, THAT LOST HIS TAIL.
DEMOCRATIC
THE N.Y. DEMOCRATS HAVE LOST THEIR HEAD BUT FOUND A TAIL.
THE END OF THE DEMOCRATS
"NO STILL HUNT" MR. TILDEN
ANOTHER GREAT QUESTION CAN A TAIL WAG WITHOUT A BODY?
WHERE IS THE HELPLESS BODY.
USUFRUCT REFORM.
LETTER EXPLAINING THAT
TWEEDS CHECK $5000
THE DEMOCRATS WANT TO SEE-MORE
LIKE A HOUND ON THE SCENT
Th. Nast.

"A grand era lies dead and buried with nothing tangible to bring it back," wrote New York Daily News *columnist Gene Ward. In the summer of 1952, the wrecker's ball had done in the bankrupt Grand Union Hotel. This 1953 architect's rendering of a promised Grand Union supermarket development was hardly consolation. Resort life at Saratoga Springs was at a low point, and her rise from the ashes would only come a dozen years later with a supermarket of another kind, the Saratoga Performing Arts Center.*

to Saratoga, however, Herbert enjoyed himself hugely and never complained. Besides, he had other ways to make money. One summer, while staying at the Grand Union, he wrote the score to his immensely popular operetta *Mlle. Modiste*. The royalties from that hit musical came in faster than even Herbert could spend them.

There were some, however, who did complain most vociferously. Spencer Trask, a wealthy stockbroker, mounted an antigambling campaign against Canfield, but it did not get very far when various church leaders of the community could not seem to see the difference between gambling at Canfield's casino or on Wall Street. Anthony Comstock, that paragon of virtue from the New York Society for the Suppression of Vice, came to Saratoga to inveigh against the evils of gambling, and a score of the more blatant establishments shuttered their doors for a few days until the Comstockian storm blew over. Joseph Pulitzer, who could have taught James Gordon Bennett a thing or two about yellow journalism, dispatched his ace reporter, Nellie Bly, to Saratoga to write an exposé of the town. Bly, as indefatigable as she was inaccurate, wrote a sizzling piece describing Saratoga as the Monte Carlo of America, "with the reckless law-breaking of Leadville (Colorado) combined with the vulgarity of the Bowery."

Although there was no immediate slowing down of the pace of Saratogian night life, the way was eventually cleared for an ambitious public official to promote himself by leading the crusade against social impropriety.

The man who offered himself was District Attorney William Jerome. Under his direction, even the venerable Casino had to stand for the ignominy of a raid. It was one thing to roust a few cardsharps, but when gentlemen were disturbed at their pleasures, it was quite another. In 1911, Canfield prudently decided to cash in his chips, which amounted to a neat $13 million. When he died three years later, his fortune had dwindled to less than $1 million. America's greatest gambling casino owner had dropped the other $12 million in the stock market.

Gambling in various forms would, of course, continue. The big sports retired to their hotel suites to play high-stakes poker games, and casino gambling continued until the 1950s, when it was finally rooted out after Congressional committee hearings under Senator Estes Kefauver established that gambling had become a principal source of income for organized crime in America. The town caught a bad case of what some of the old-timers called "Kefauver fever." Public gambling, except for horse racing and later the New York State Lottery, passed from the Saratoga scene.

Something of the community fled when Canfield retired. Perhaps it was just as well. The times were changing and, reluctantly, Saratoga had to change with them. Americans still knew how to throw their cash about, but the rigors of the two world wars and the scrutiny of the Internal Revenue Service had a dampening effect. Rich people continued to come for the racing season with a somewhat rougher element trailing in their wake. But instead of brash public brigands of the stripe of Jay Gould and John Gates, now they were quieter men such as Arnold Rothstein and Lucky Luciano.

Increasingly, the work of Saratoga became the province of the corporation and the government bureaucracy. Both did valuable work for the community. When it appeared for a time that commercial interests might suck the springs dry of their carbonic-acid gasses and use them in the manufacture of carbonated beverages, a civic group headed by Spenser Trask and George Peabody spearheaded a movement to have New York State buy up most of the important springs in the area and preserve them for their therapeutic uses. In 1929, New York governor Franklin Delano Roosevelt appointed a special commission headed by Bernard Baruch to make a comprehensive study and survey of the springs, which led to the establishment of a state spa. No one could deny the importance of these developments, but they do not have quite the same drama as Jim Fisk making an expensive fool of himself dressed up in a Zouave uniform.

One by one, the old mammoth hotels gave way to smaller-scaled accommodations. The United States Hotel fell into a slow decline and finally went under the wrecker's ball in 1946. The Grand Union was shuttered six years later.

Saratoga survives, of course. Fine architecture, a salubrious climate, large expenditures of cash, and good horse flesh should be enough for any community. But the old Saratoga, the Saratoga where Diamond Jim Brady dreamed his gaudiest dreams, was gone forever.

Still, as they were fond of saying in the society columns of the day, "a grand time was had by all."

SARATOGA SCHOTTISCH
AT SARATOGA
ARRANGED FOR THE
Piano Forte
OHANN MUNCK
HORACE WATERS
Boston G. P. REED & Co
5
JUST ONE
SARATOGA
MARCH
TWO STEP

Chapter II

ARTS AND ARCHITECTURE

by Jennifer Dunning

"There is too much of architectural glory; but the American likes grandeur, and here he has it, in a profusion perfectly dazzling."

From *Saratoga Illustrated: The Visitor's Guide to Saratoga Springs*, 1882

The air of Saratoga Springs is "full of music and the atmosphere of harmony," an observer once wrote of this upstate New York town. For two months each summer, Saratoga reverberates with dance, music, and opera. Glamorous ballerinas waddle up and down Saratoga's main street in July, their legs and feet turned out to 45 degrees. Humming musicians and conversing actors wander heedlessly across Saratoga's broad central avenue. Cars throng the normally tranquil side streets as fans head to a concert by the Kinks, perhaps, or Liza Minnelli or the Bama Band. But Saratogians take it all in stride with typically accepting grace. It is not for nothing that they have lived for over a century with visiting exotics drawn by the town's mineral baths, its gambling, its Thoroughbred racing, and now its reputation as a lively and exceptionally civilized summer festival of the arts.

For Saratoga has served as a summer home to the New York City Ballet and the Philadelphia Orchestra since 1966, when the Saratoga Performing Arts Center (SPAC) opened on the green slopes and lawns of the Saratoga State Park, just south of town. One of the world's largest outdoor theaters, the center now plays host as well to the New York City Opera, which in 1987 became its third resident performing-arts company, thanks to a grant of $2.5 million from the H. Schaffer Foundation of Schenectady—the single largest gift ever presented to SPAC and one that SPAC itself will attempt to match. The center is also host to the Newport Jazz Festival–Saratoga, with popular music groups moving into the house on other nights, and modern and off-beat dance companies drawing audiences to the handsome Little Theatre

PRECEDING PAGES

Summer evenings in Saratoga have always been musically alive: from a schottische at the dawn of the Victorian era to a two-step of Edwardian times; from the allegro of Doring's Military Band to the pianissimo of Ormandy's Philadelphia Orchestra, the echoes of many a midsummer-night's dream are to be heard here.

OPPOSITE

By 1880, Saratoga's hotels offered thousands of first-class rooms, 900 of which were in the Grand Union, directly facing Congress Park. A modern Urban Cultural Park offers legal protection and economic support to architecture born in Saratoga's earlier heydays.

Clog dancing to Appalachian music, street performers liven up Saratoga's Broadway.

nearby. And Saratoga itself has become one of the nation's most popular summer festival towns.

Shop fronts along Broadway, Saratoga's main thoroughfare, bristle with ballet paraphernalia in July. Music books and artifacts jostle for space in August with horse jewelry of every description and "Saratoga Crying Towels" for losers at the track. "It's so difficult to compete," Herbert A. Chesbrough, president and executive director of SPAC, says. "We're fighting one hundred years of history."

The atmosphere at SPAC changes with each attraction. At Newport Jazz Festival–Saratoga time, the lawns and woods become a single, rambling community of amateur saxophonists, buyers of macramé, and campers united by their common love of the music. They fly and drive to Saratoga, often from great distances, to attend the two-day festival, an extension of the famed jazz festival in Newport, Rhode Island. Friends arrange to take turns in theater and lawn seats, enjoying the shade and relative cool and comfort of the seats inside the amphitheater, then sprawling in the sun on the lawn beyond, where the cheaper tickets are. If the listening gets dull, there are crafts-fair tents to wander through. And there are always new friends to be made as food and drinks are shared on hot afternoons and impromptu jam sessions burst forth in the parking lot. One gets to know one's neighbors in the fifteen-hour day most jazz fans spend at the festival.

It is a little more formal at a City Ballet matinee a few weeks later. There are picnics everywhere. Little girls wear flowing summer dresses, and babies in bonnets loll in their strollers. Lawn chairs are set out early and determinedly. But the otherwise lazy pace into the amphitheater quickens as the post horn sounds in racetrack fashion. "Balanchine hit on the idea," Chesbrough says, referring to the late George Balanchine, a founder of City Ballet, its chief choreographer, and an important influence in the planning of SPAC. "He liked the sound of the bugle. It's something I keep because of him. The start of the race. The call to the post. He had a rather interesting sense of humor."

Motherly ushers rush to help a woman pushing a man in a wheelchair. "They are our greatest public relations experts," Chesbrough says of the ushers, who are all volunteers. "They talk about us all year in their communities." The ushers, like a good seventy percent of the ballet audiences, come from areas within an hour's drive from Saratoga.

A little boy blows soap bubbles out across the lawn as the performance begins and the dancers romp through Jerome Robbins's *Interplay*, dressed in dance clothes the colors of bright Ice Slurpies. Some in the lawn audience are clearly working on their tans. Others take solemn notes on the performance. Some watch from the shade underneath an entrance ramp, and parents and children chomp companionably on sandwiches and raisins.

That night, there is a performance by the experimentalist Laura Dean Dancers and Musicians at the Little Theatre. Erected in the 1930s, the elegant building is part of a formal vista that includes a reflecting pool, cloisters, and walkways at a slight distance from SPAC's newer amphitheater. There is a varied reception inside for Dean's fast-flowing, geometrically patterned dances and their throbbingly percussive scores. "Whoo! Hot!" one teenager exclaims during intermission. "What kind of ballet is this, anyway?" a man asks plaintively of his wife.

"I know Laura Dean is kind of a shock to someone who's only seen *Coppélia*," Chesbrough says. "But we have to present every kind of dance in the spectrum. And I find people have a little more open minds than they sometimes think they do." Attendance at modern dance performances at the Little Theatre was about seventy-five percent of capacity in 1986, with comparable seats at the amphitheater's ballet performances selling out most nights. Chesbrough dreams of enlarging the festival's dance component so that audiences can see three different companies over a single weekend.

The opening of the National Museum of Dance in the state park complex in July 1986 has added to SPAC's status as a dance center. Located in the refurbished Washington Baths, the museum has a welcoming, light-filled Beaux-Arts foyer with two spacious exhibition rooms beyond. In its first summer, the museum housed a lavish and instructive exhibit of costumes worn through the years by dancers in noted American ballet companies, as well as a succinct photographic history of American modern dance and a show of the drawings and notes of postmodernist choreographers and artists in dance. In 1987, the exhibitions included a show of dance portraits by the photographer Kenn Duncan.

The Twilight Chamber Series is presented on the SPAC grounds free to ticket holders before performances during the ballet and orchestra seasons in a small, flower-fringed gazebo across the green from the amphitheater. String

Overnighting jazz-festival fans spread their tents before the State Park's Hall of Springs.

music performed by the Philarte Quartet serves as a sweet introduction to an evening performance by the Philadelphia Orchestra, attended by the most casually elegant of the audiences.

Outside the theater, lit cigarettes and picnic candles give the lawn the look of a rarefied campsite, though some study musical scores by the light of those candles. Cigar smoke drifts aromatically through the air, offering an odd, synesthetic counterpoint to the edgy and astringent nostalgia of Virgil Thomson's *Five Songs by William Blake*, conducted by Dennis Russell Davies, principal conductor and classical-music program director at SPAC.

Inside, a father nods to his bored-looking young son as the music winds around them. One of the center's recent innovations has been the creation of a resident-composer program, featuring Philip Glass in 1985, Lou Harrison in 1986, and William Bolcom in 1987. Designed to encourage appreciation of contemporary American music, the program doesn't address Chesbrough's other worries. The jazz festivals are the only season programs to draw a racially mixed audience. And attendees at concert music are getting older, Chesbrough observes, as they are in the concert halls of New York City.

He estimates ballet audiences to be in their thirties, forties, and fifties, while the orchestra audiences tend to be in their fifties through seventies. "We are all going to have to change to survive," he says of the music programming. "Wouldn't it be interesting," he adds, "to draw on the latest technology and give concert audiences large video-screen close-ups of the conductor and musicians at work?"

The lawn of the Saratoga Performing Arts Center is an idyllic picnic spot during the two-month season.

When SPAC opened, on July 8, 1966, the workmen who built the theater were invited to a special preview performance and greeted the ballet spectacle before them with steadily increasing interest. But it was not until the following night, at the official opening, that the town and business leaders who had worked so hard to make the center a reality were able to get a foretaste of their success in making Saratoga a summer capital of the arts.

The night was cloudy but pleasant. The audience, as one observer noted, had an air of opulence, though newspaper photographs of the event reveal men and women in fine evening wear pausing like shy, awed adolescents on the grassy hill leading down to the new amphitheater. Captains of local industry voiced hopes to wandering reporters about the new center's possible effect on business. And then the ballet began, and with it a real sense of the fitness of this new home for art.

The first original full-evening ballet created in America, George Balanchine's *A Midsummer Night's Dream* had the right ingredients for the setting as well as the occasion. The park's tall pines encircled a pinpoint stage forest below filled with darting human butterflies and tiny, bobbing fireflies danced by children, with lovers warring through rolling mists, and with lolloping bumpkins who might have wandered onto the stage from a wood very like the one beyond the stage. A beautiful queen, reclining in a bower made of seashell, epitomized the otherwordly creatures who would soon invade the town inhabited by their mortal audiences.

"At Saratoga," the dance critic Byron Belt has written, "it always

The 5,000-seat theater hosts big bands, and the Gazebo offers gentle jazz for a July afternoon during the two days of Newport Jazz at Saratoga.

seems that there is a special touch of moon-struck magic to the dreaming midsummer's night. Ballet may be an imperial art, but it is at one with nature, too, and the blend of elegance and the wonders of the lush New York countryside seem to make for an ideal union."

From the first days of its conception, early in the 1960s, the performing arts festival and center were seen, at least in part, as a way of reviving the sagging economy of the once-thriving town. "It is not an exaggeration, I think, to say that tonight marks a rebirth for Saratoga," Laurance S. Rockefeller said in his opening-night speech. A local newspaperman put it more colorfully. "Saratoga Springs (pop. 16,630), like the matron under the mudpack, seems to be getting new life," Robert G. Case wrote in the *Syracuse Herald-Journal.*

By the late 1950s, Saratoga had become known solely as a racing town—and only for a single month each year. Talk began in 1961 about establishing a summer performing-arts center. Governor Nelson A. Rockefeller was interested, and local leading families and patrons of the arts were enthusiastic. A plan was developed by a group of five prominent citizens led by Newman E. Wait, Jr., president of the Adirondack Trust Company, and Harold G. Wilm, the state conservation commissioner, whose authority over the state parks, including the spa at Saratoga, made him a natural choice for directing the development of the center.

"He'd studied violin as a boy, thank God," the late Richard P. Leach,

FESTIVAL

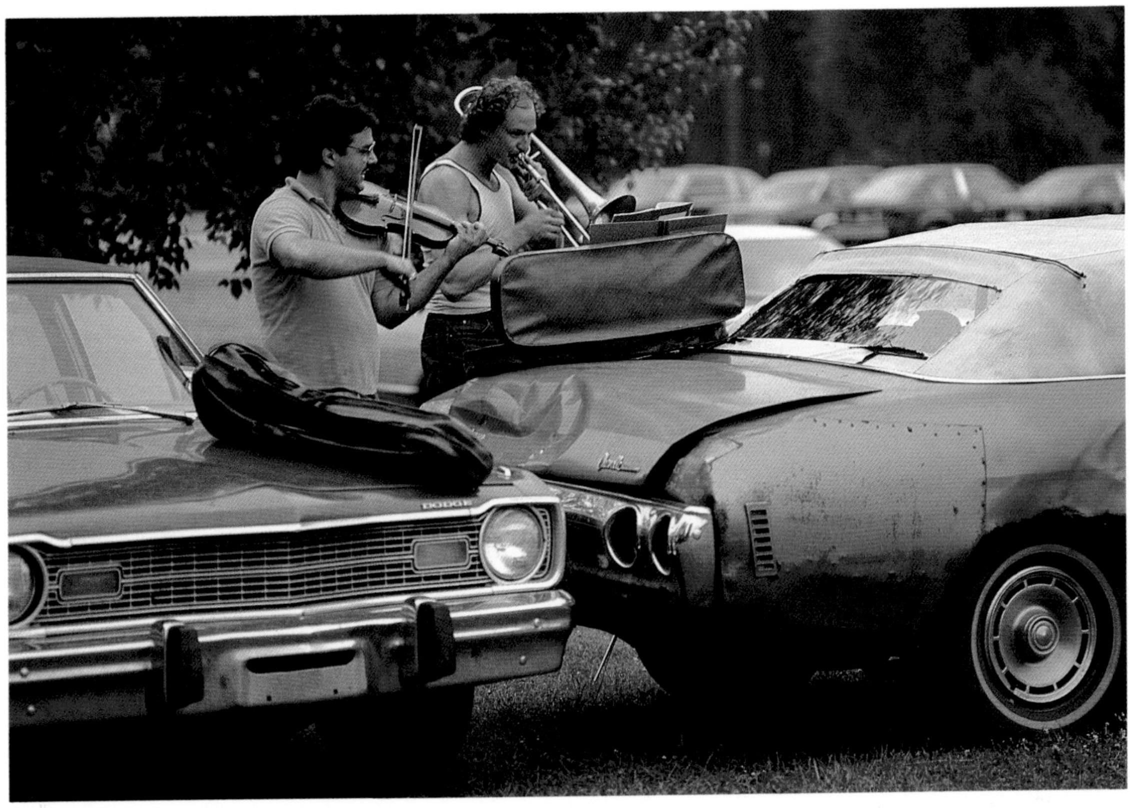

While Gladys Knight and the Pipps play the main stage, two old pals enjoy their parking lot jam.

who also helped to shape the center, said of Wilm. "And Pete Wait was Mr. Saratoga in the very real sense." Leach's varied and extensive experience in classical music management and as a founding director of the Aspen Festival and first program director of Lincoln Center led him to be named executive director of the Saratoga Performing Arts Center in 1964.

The center was seen as serving the Capital Area, which includes Albany, Amsterdam, Schenectady, Troy, Glens Falls, and Gloversville, all about thirty miles from the center by the highways that form a network at the outskirts of Saratoga. Vollmer Associates of New York was selected to plan and execute the installation. The dimensions and layout of the theater were determined with the continuing advice of the New York City Ballet and the Philadelphia Orchestra, the center's first two summer residents. "George came into the picture very totalitarianly," Leach recalled, affectionately, of Balanchine and his concern for the stage surface. "It was the floor, the floor, the floor."

The ground breaking for this "imperial theater in the Empire State," as Lincoln Kirstein, cofounder with Balanchine of the City Ballet, was to call the $4.6 million project, was held on June 30, 1964. The largest contribution—$1.3 million—was given by the Rockefeller Brothers Fund, and Saratogians and New York State contributed $1 million each, with additional money coming from residents of the Capital Area and other cities in the state. Leach stated that the largest area contributors were doctors and dentists, and that the "rich and ritzy racing people of August" outdid themselves in an effort spearheaded by Mrs. Ogden Phipps.

With the Philadelphia Orchestra's arrival in August, chamber music flows from the Gazebo and symphonic practice sessions serenade nearby golfers.

The first City Ballet season lasted through July 31. Chosen as a SPAC resident when the New York Philharmonic proved uninterested in the project, the Philadelphia Orchestra moved into the center on August 4 with an all-Beethoven program that included *The Consecration of the House*, conducted by Eugene Ormandy. In typically congenial Saratoga fashion, the Philadelphia performers were joined by members of three area choruses. The City Ballet gave twenty-one performances and the Philadelphia Orchestra fourteen, a ratio that has persisted into the 1980s. The first season also included performances of chamber music by the DePasquale Quartet, the Philadelphia Woodwind Quintet, and the Philadelphia Brass Ensemble.

The theater seats 5,103 inside the open-backed auditorium, with room for 7,000 on the lawn. The stage is 80 feet wide by 60 feet deep, with a proscenium 30 feet 10 inches high. Backstage, there are 87 rooms on three levels. One of the two rehearsal studios is stage-size. And the dance floors Balanchine worried so about? They are multilayered and made of Saratoga yellow pine in a basketweave design, covered in gray linoleum, which was developed by Balanchine and Ronald Bates for maximum resiliency.

The theater's acoustics successfully overcame the problems posed by an open-air arena and one that is twice as large as the optimal size for good concert-hall sound. Paul Veneklasen, the theater's acoustical consultant, achieved this through the use of canvas baffles, wood side-wall panels, and a stage canopy that reflects sound downward and out into the audience—all giving the stage frame the look of a nun's wimple in stately disarray.

KEEP OFF

But this was not enough for Ormandy. A stream, part of the park's magnificent Geyser Creek, runs by the back of the theater—a stream, incidentally, in which a City Ballet dancer once caught seven trout, which he cooked on a hibachi and served backstage. In a conversation Leach remembered well, Ormandy insisted that the stream be dammed.

"What is that?" the conductor asked.

"A waterfall," Leach answered.

"Ormandy said it would interfere—with the pianissimo in *Afternoon of a Faun* or whatever," Leach recalled. Suggestions were made for silencing the stream, among them smothering it in canvas or damming it upstream by means of a floodgate operated by a backstage switch that could be flipped for a three-hour period of silence.

Balanchine arrived later. "He sat on a sill in one of the private dressing rooms," Leach said. The room was designed for Balanchine and Ormandy, but Balanchine never used it, saying he preferred to dress with "the boys" or male principal dancers. But the season had not yet started, and he and Leach were contemplating the company's new summer home.

"Silence was [Balanchine's] other native tongue," Leach said. But he loved the sound of falling water. Hearing it backstage, he asked Leach if that were the waterfall "Mr. Ormandy" would turn off. "Yes, Mr. B.," Leach said. "Dick," Balanchine responded, "much better we turn off Ormandy." Today, the waterfall is dammed for orchestra and opera performances but not for the ballet, in an operation that is performed with a series of manual valves.

Not only does the Saratoga Performing Arts Center (SPAC) host jazz, opera, ballet, and symphony, it also presents road shows.

FOLLOWING PAGES

Nearing its 25th season, SPAC enjoys a composer-in-residence program, inaugurated by Phillip Glass (pp. 72–73). The New York City Ballet annually presents such modern classics as George Balanchine's Jewels *(pp. 74–75). Touring artists like Rudolf Nureyev practice through the afternoon at SPAC (pp. 76–77) before an evening's dance concert, while nearby the next generation of prima ballerinas is training at the New York State Summer School of the Arts under the watchful eye of dance mistress Olga (pp. 78–79).*

115
116
117

SPAC

The center has its enduring legends, many of which have to do with the weather. Pete Seeger once invited his lawn audience into the theater to escape a drizzle, and *Dances at a Gathering* was once performed during a thunder-and-lightning storm, with clouds of mist pouring across the stage and a sopping Robert Irving, the company's music director, playing doggedly through the Chopin piano score. Then there was the distinguished citizen of Saratoga who, unfamiliar with classical ballet, sat happily through *A Midsummer Night's Dream* on opening night but was dismayed by the ballet's central pas de deux. It seemed such a good dance. He turned to a friend, and asked, "Why didn't they have the whole company do it?"

Such a novelty has never occurred at the center, but just about everything else has in SPAC's first twenty years. New works have been created for center seasons, among them Balanchine's 1974 *Coppélia*. "Saratoga asked me to do something for children," the choreographer once explained. "There are twenty-four in the third act. I like the name. It is very appealing and is a better title for a ballet than something like 'Tragedy in the Night.'" Some offerings, like the "special events" that bring popular star solo performers to the stage, were devised to help meet deficits that have recurred despite a steadily growing audience and the state's agreement in 1967 to become the center's landlord. Ballet is expensive to present, though it is a more steady and reliable draw than the orchestra. Harry Belafonte was the first of the special-event performers, in 1967. In June 1985, the Grateful Dead set the all-time attendance record for a single event with a crowd of 40,231.

Hal Holbrook's 1967 presentation of *Mark Twain Tonight* was the first theater offering at the center, which has also presented musical theater and classical and contemporary drama by such groups as the Circle Repertory Company, the Abbey Theater, the Central Children's Theater of Moscow, the Empire State Youth Theater Institute, and Syracuse Stage. John Houseman and his troupe of young actors, known variously as the Acting Company and City Center Acting Company, were the center's third resident from 1972 to 1980.

Film festivals were presented from 1967 to 1977. Modern dance was introduced in 1969, and the José Limòn, Twyla Tharp, and Murray Louis dance companies were resident in 1985, 1986, and 1987, respectively. Jazz was performed in two-day Newport, Kool, Upstate, and New York Jazz Festivals from 1978 on. There have also been festivals of folk and country music, American song, and Russian music and dance. In 1987, SPAC and the City Ballet initiated the Little Theatre Choreography Project, a workshop featuring dancers from the City Ballet–affiliated School of American Ballet. The D'Oyly Carte Opera Company and Lake George Opera Company have also appeared at SPAC. And the center has played host to countless community activities over the years, from high school and college graduation ceremonies to Mother's Day programs.

One of the most colorful of presentations was a series of exhibitions of classical horseback riding on the park green, sponsored in the early 1970s by the American Dressage Institute, which also established a riding school in Saratoga in connection with the summer festival during the early 1960s. But youngsters bustling about the Skidmore College campus during the summer of 1986 were learning the equally exotic arts of dance, music, and theater.

Dance, in particular, seems to burst out in Saratoga in the summer, like the grass and tall clover that push through a stretch of broken stone walkway on Woodlawn, a street that runs through an area where great summer mansions, called "cottages," once flourished. A few blocks before the sidewalk turns to brick, then slab, then country weeds under tall, hovering trees, one passes the stern old headquarters of the Saratoga Elks Club. Move through the dark wood hallways on a July morning, by the empty meeting rooms and up flights of stairs to the top floor, which has the feel of an airy cupola floating out over the trees and hills of Saratoga, and you may find a ballet class in progress.

Sometimes traditions collide in Saratoga. Elisabeth Carroll, the tiny, chic veteran of several major American ballet companies and now a leading teacher in town, listens as a student tells her before class of a workshop with Laura Dean, one of a series offered locally each summer by SPAC with its guest companies. "Well," the student says a little dubiously, "we walked on a line backwards and forwards and spun in a circle."

Classical ballet is also taught by Oleg Briansky and Mireille Briane, teachers in New York City, who have operated a summer ballet school in Saratoga since 1966. During the summer of 1986, they offered an innovative participatory survey of international ballet styles in a hectic, six-day teachers' seminar held in a dance studio at Skidmore College. Teachers and students from across the continent worked through classes, discussions, and the learning of a signature dance in each style, first with Dinna Bjorn of the Royal Danish Ballet, an expert in the nineteenth-century style of August Bournonville, then with Elena Tchernicheva, a ballet mistress at American Ballet Theater who came to teach the Soviet ballet system devised by Agrippina Vaganova, and then with Suki Schorer.

Schorer is a former member of City Ballet and a teacher at the company-affiliated School of American Ballet in New York City. Observed at work, she darted with her charges through a methodical but vivid learning of a variation from Balanchine's *Divertimento No. 15*, which City Ballet was performing that week at SPAC. She referred often to Balanchine, quoting, with affectionate admiration, his gnomic, yeasty prescriptions for good stage dancing. Soon Balanchine's spirit seemed to permeate the room. "A horse step!" the class pianist murmured as the dancers scooped legs up and out through a high-stepping "pas de cheval." "He must have choreographed that up here."

The possibilities for chaos are unlimited in this corner of Skidmore's Field House, where the New York State Summer School of the Arts is also in session in late June, July, and August. Here, in a pristine new sports and dance complex, selected students from high schools across the state participate in intensive four-week sessions in their field of expertise, sponsored by the State Education Department and SPAC. Students in ballet, orchestral studies, and theater work at Skidmore with members of the City Ballet, the Philadelphia Orchestra, and the Circle Repertory Company of New York.

Competitions for New York State's Summer School of the Arts bring top students to Saratoga for a memorable learning experience with the professional companies that perform there each summer.

Summer schools in choral studies, film, and media and visual arts are held elsewhere in the state.

At none of the summer school's divisions are the ties between study and the stage so glamorously evident as in the School of Dance. Heather Watts is a principal dancer with the New York City Ballet. But in Saratoga, in the summer of 1986, she spent most of her days at Skidmore as artistic director of the dance division. Surveying the children assembled before her each day, she judged with a gentle but firmly authoritative eye. None of the sixty girls and boys, who wore name tags and worked before a small audience of faculty members and teachers, was at school to learn deportment. "The idea is to replicate the life of a dancer," Mary Daley, administrator of the arts school program, says. "Do they really want to put in this time, or be with their peers? They go to performances every night here, then start class at 9 A.M. each morning." Two of the students fell asleep the other night at a performance, she notes, huddled in blankets in their seats.

In addition to their technique classes, the children learn classical dances and study ballet history, injury prevention, and jazz and character dancing. As with the other divisions, the program aims to give youngsters an idea of how to go about preparing for their art. "We identify upstate New York kids who have potential but wouldn't know how to go about going to New York," Daley says. "We found Robert Lyon through the program." Lyon, a native of Schenectady, went on to study at the School of American Ballet. He won the school's prestigious first annual Mae L. Wien Award in 1987 and is often mentioned as a highly promising young professional. The ballet students, between twelve and eighteen years old, tend to be slightly younger than students in the other divisions. But all are selected in statewide auditions for the program, founded in 1970.

Sleek young colts, the ballet students arrive at least a half hour before class to stretch and warm up on their own. The young musicians who pile cheerfully into the Field House in late July are a motleyer crew. A cheerleader here, a punk "Mohawk" there, they arrive a few minutes before their classes, lugging large and small instrument cases. Full-throated orchestral music surges out now, supplanting the tinkling classroom pianos of the ballet school.

Here, youngsters study the theory, history, and literature of music, and play in string, wind, and full orchestral ensembles coached by "the Philly boys," as one school administrator refers to the first-chair Philadelphia Orchestra musicians who work with the students. Provided, like the ballet students, with free tickets to SPAC performances, the young musicians hear some of the music they are learning played by the orchestra, and they themselves give regular preperformance concerts at the center. They also have the opportunity actually to experience contemporary music and to work with professional musicians.

"What we try to do is work with them on orchestra parts," Norman Carol, concertmaster of the Philadelphia Orchestra and a longtime teacher of violin at the summer school, said of the students. "And we show them what playing in an orchestra is about. Unfortunately, some have had such limited opportunities that you end up teaching them how to play violin. But these kids are like musical sponges." Three participants in the summer school have gone on to perform with the Philadelphia Orchestra. "We don't go to Saratoga with the idea of finding players, but we can influence what kind of music college they go to and tell them how important it is to find good private instructors.

"You have to be very flexible. Their problems are all in different areas. The idea is that when you work with one student you make sure everybody is aware of the problems. I have students play alone. I don't say anything. I have others comment, though not in a malicious way. They spend an enormous amount of time away from their teachers. It's important for the coach to show them how to practice. They become aware of what I react to. And they react."

The students tend initially to be shy. "But after a while they nail you after class. I think all the orchestra members try to be as honest as possible —to show what an orchestra player's life is like and what equipment musicians should have." Students sometimes have naive ideas about the rigorous and competitive life of the professional musician. One frequent question is whether the high school music "challenge system," where back-row orchestra players can simply ask for a chance to prove themselves up front, is in operation at the Philadelphia Orchestra.

Extreme self-possession distinguishes the students in the acting school, though it wavers slightly in the morning movement classes. In the afternoon scene-presentation class, one young actress even allows herself a stagy fit of nerves. "You have a performance tonight," Nancy Donahue, the class teacher and a member of the Circle Repertory Company, admonished briskly, offering an unambiguous lesson in professionalism.

The summer school music program runs concurrently with the Philadelphia Orchestra's three-week season. The first-chair cellist of "The Philadelphia" is this young man's coach.

There was to be a reading at Skidmore that night of scenes by such playwrights as Jean Giraudoux, Neil Simon, and Wendy Wasserstein, worked on by the students in a month that also included classes in acting technique and voice. Two other students finished a scene from Ferenc Molnar's *Liliom* and learned another lesson, this time about the vital process of acting. "What can you tell me about this?" Donahue asked the two. "It's not like last night," one student said wistfully. "Last night was very good," Donahue said. "This was not so much because you were thinking about last night. Don't try to find exactly the same execution. Just the same actions."

And there were moments of sudden, unexpected magic in the classroom. Two young women began a scene as the innocent girlfriends in Horton Foote's *A Young Lady of Property*. Donahue settled back with the rest of the class to watch. There was an instant of silence after the two finished a scene played with unforgettable, youthful poignancy. This was an acting class, however, and the moment came to a neat and fitting end as Donahue made a gentle suggestion about clarifying the "geography" of the scene.

But there is more theater to Saratoga than the goings-on at SPAC and in its classrooms and studios, for Saratoga was once a theater town. Its history as such has almost vanished, existing chiefly in scattered references in the books and other holdings of the Saratoga History Room at the city library, which is located in Congress Park, on the site of the famed Congress Hall Hotel. But the ghosts do linger on.

Saratoga's earliest theatrical entrepreneur seems to have been a Mr. Vilallave, a tightrope walker, gymnast, and sleight-of-hand artist who built a small playhouse in 1819, possibly just off Broadway opposite Washington Street. Vilallave abandoned it a few years later, formed a successful stock company in a second, very beautiful theater, and settled for another few years into a third and last theater on Caroline Street. A nineteenth-century theater chronicler recalls having seen Master Burke, "a star of the times," perform there one summer in the early 1830s in *The Tragedy of Douglass* and *The Irish Schoolteacher*. "A traveling lecturer gave an exhibition of laughing gas" there as well, to "a moderate audience."

The opening of some twelve theaters between 1824 and 1880 is recorded—the last two of which, interestingly, were engaged almost nightly in the winter but far less consistently in summer months. The next theater of note to open was the Spa Summer Theater, now the Little Theatre, one of several buildings erected during the 1930s in the state preserve that is now the state park surrounding SPAC. Designed originally as a lecture hall for the medical students associated with the hydrotherapy clinical and research facilities on the grounds, the five-hundred-seat proscenium auditorium began to be used as a theater in 1936, when a young repertory company played there during summer months. Ethel Barrymore was one of the stars who appeared with the company, and performers visiting Saratoga delivered short, informal talks to audiences before performances. Musicals largely replaced drama there in the 1950s, but by the early 1960s audiences had dwindled and the theater fell into disrepair. It was revived with the opening of SPAC in 1966.

SPAC rekindled a tradition when it leased the building for out-of-season performances to the Home Made Theater, considered one of the most promising and accomplished of the thirty or so amateur theater companies operating in the Capital Area. Amateur theatricals have a long history in Saratoga. Histrionic Hall, a leading Saratoga theater in the mid-nineteenth century, housed a group of nonprofessionals who played there for several years. The Comedy Club, established in 1911 and active until 1917 and then only sporadically after that, presented a number of plays written by Charles Brackett, the son of State Senator Edgar Truman Brackett and later a noted Hollywood producer; Frank Sullivan, the humorist and essayist known as "the sage of Saratoga," was also an active member.

Amateur musical groups also had a long history here, flourishing as church choirs and in concerts given at local clubs and schools, among the latter the early twentieth-century forerunner to Skidmore College. The town even had its own *Saratoga Musical Monthly* magazine during the 1880s. Bands, orchestras, and wandering hurdy-gurdies were everywhere in July and August.

Popular concert sites included the track, Congress Park, and Hathorn Spring. Ernestine Schumann-Heink sang in Congress Park, as did Cesaeretta Jones, known as "the black Patti," and "Blind Tom." At the height of the season, visitors could attend two or three band concerts a day in the park.

Francis "Frank" Johnson, a black musician and composer who performed with his band in Saratoga from 1821 into the 1840s, helped to escort

visiting dignitaries into town in marches that could not have been too different in spirit from Balanchine's somewhat bemused ride into Saratoga in a surrey, serenaded by the Avant Garde Drum and Bugle Corps, on "George Balanchine Day" in 1977. "The groves and spacious halls of Saratoga," noted an admirer of Johnson, who composed popular dance music named after the town, "resounded with the notes of his enchanting bugle and violin."

Most musical activities were centered around the hotels. There were parlor concerts at many of the more successful establishments. Victor Herbert's orchestra performed regularly at the Grand Union, and a group of musicians from the Boston Symphony played at the United States Hotel. Similarly, musicians from the City Ballet orchestra now play in impromptu ensembles at the Adelphi Hotel, which has also provided an occasional home for the Ynternal Amateurs Ballet, a wickedly satirical local dance group headed by Peter Anastos.

Then there were Johnson's "celebrated hops and balls" at Congress Hall, the first resort hotel in America to employ a band or orchestra for its guests. Those balls were important events. The "ladies only had 36 hours to prepare" for one held in honor of General Ulysses S. Grant, a chronicler of Saratoga society observed, and guests readied themselves for the balls by working with dancing masters provided by the hotels.

Saratoga also had its flower festivals and historical pageants, and odd diversions like the weekly appearances of Madame Carlotta, known as "the intrepid lady," who rose above Congress Park in a balloon every summer

Saratoga is nurturing its own future through support of programs in music, dance, theater, and choral studies.

FOLLOWING PAGES
Onstage rehearsal at SPAC fine-tunes wind duets, percussion crescendos, and tympany accents for the summer students' graduation concert.

IGROSCHENOPER
Ein Stück mit Musik in einem Vorspiel und acht Bildern
Nr. 1. OVERTURE
KURT WEILL

PRECEDING PAGES
In the words of Frank Leslie's Illustrated Newspaper *of August 28, 1875, Saratoga "is an oasis of repose in the desert of our American hurry. Life is leisurely there, and business is amusement. It is a perpetual festival."*
THIS PAGE
Chef to that festival was George Crum. Saratoga legend, accepted as fact, traces the potato chip to its birth in Crum's kitchen. The world now munches on his thinner-than-thin Saratoga chips.
OPPOSITE
The lighter-than-air bravura of Madame Carlotta entranced Congress Park visitors in the 1880s. Every summer Sunday, the faithful flocked—and she flew.

Sunday from 1884 to 1889. Films came to Saratoga in 1897, when the two-hundred-fifty-seat Edisonia Theater opened on Broadway, presenting "kinetoscopes," a "curio museum," and a "cosmorama." Movie houses sprang up and thrived through the 1930s. And film stars were a regular feature of Saratoga summers, particularly during "opening week" in August, appearing at bazaars and at the "lake houses" that had flourished since the mid-nineteenth century around Saratoga Lake—restaurants and clubs known for everything from the invention of the potato chip to regular presentations of shows by female impersonators. Zoe Flanagan, the proprietor, with her daughter, Zoe Ann Coleman, of the Rip Van Dam Hotel, remembers children staring goggle-eyed as the men walked through Saratoga in full make-up.

A half-century later, Saratoga culture has become somewhat more sedate. But it was one of Saratoga's richest cultural institutions that paved the way for today's activities. Unique in its day, the Yaddo artists' retreat began in 1932 to present programs designed to expose connoisseurs, its own resident musicians, and some visitors to the best and most interesting in modern American music. Initiated by Elizabeth Ames, Yaddo's formidable but devoted director for forty-five years, the music festivals were discontinued in 1952 because they seemed to draw resources and attention from Yaddo's main purpose, which was to provide free time and space for uninterrupted work for writers, composers, and visual artists.

"There is no program, no structure, no obligation here," Curtis Har-

Skidmore students—on point or on horseback—have graced Saratoga's life year round. At first, the school's campus was expanded by buying up Victorian mansions. In recent years, Skidmore men and women have moved onto a modern campus on North Broadway.

nack, Yaddo's recently retired director, said of the artists' retreat in 1986. About one hundred sixty-five "guests" are selected each year by panels of peers for visits of from ten days to two months, with thirty-five to forty people staying in the summer at any one time and ten to fifteen in the winter. All they are expected to do is to concentrate on their work for at least seven hours a day and be sufficiently sociable to live and dine with. "The artist has to feel that what he or she is doing is not just OK but nurtured as special and important. These people are treated, often for the first time in their lives, as if what they're doing is worthy of respect. Here, suddenly, what they're doing is honored."

The interchange among guests is another important part of the Yaddo experience. "America is a very lonely country for most artists," Harnack said. Although some guests find it difficult to cope with such attention, most wish never to leave Yaddo. "We had one woman, a painter, say she was going to hide in the woods. I told her not to do that, that it had been tried before."

Yaddo's famed Rose Garden, laid out in 1899 in the formal Italian style, is the only part of the retreat that is open to the public. Some twenty thousand people visit the gardens each year, many peering into the distance for a glimpse of some wandering, abstracted writer, famed or otherwise. Known and unknown have worked at Yaddo, whose roster includes an extraordinary number of American cultural figures, from Milton Avery and James Baldwin to Virgil Thomson and Eudora Welty. Noted musical scores and books have been created at Yaddo, among them the composer David del

Tredici's *Final Alice* and Carson McCullers's *The Member of the Wedding*, William Carlos Williams's *Paterson*, James T. Farrell's *Studs Lonigan*, and Katherine Anne Porter's *Ship of Fools*.

The Victorian Age novelty, the safety bicycle, propelled a float in the 1890s version of the Rose Bowl Parade: The Floral Fête. When frivolous processions were not filling Broadway, serious ones were. Horse-drawn coaches of all description passed parents and comely daughters in continuous review for the benefit of potential suitors.

Little has changed here over the years since Spencer Trask, a New York City financier, bought the property in 1881 and he and his wife, Katrina, renovated its Italian-villa-style wooden house. The estate was named Yaddo, legend goes, when Christina, the oldest Trask daughter, connected the shadow of pine trees on the estate with the dark mourning clothes of the family, which had just lost one of its children. "Call it Yaddo, Mama, for it makes poetry!" Christina Trask is said to have exclaimed. "Yaddo, shadow—shadow, Yaddo! It sounds like shadow but it's not going to be shadow." As Katrina Trask began publishing novels and poetry and writing plays, the mansion became a mecca for distinguished writers and artists drawn to the Trask house parties and masques.

Tragedy dogged the family, however: sometime before 1888, Alan, one of the four Trask children, died; in 1888 Christina and Spencer Jr. died; and a year later the last child, Katrina, died. Three years after that, the Yaddo mansion burned down. A new one was finished in 1893, designed by William Halsey Wood in the style of a late Victorian English country house, with Italian Renaissance, Gothic, and Moorish touches. The Louis Comfort Tiffany and Charles Lamb studios created the stained- and leaded-glass windows of the mansion, which was filled with period pieces and ecclesiastic furniture from Europe. In 1900, the Trasks created a corporation to preserve

THIS PAGE
A ca. 1890 portrait of Spencer Trask, whose estate, Yaddo, is now an artists' retreat. Trask was a financier and also an amateur photographer.
OPPOSITE
Katrina Trask, photographed in 1887 by her husband, Spencer

Yaddo as a permanent retreat in which to write, paint, sculpt, and compose music. The retreat was opened in 1926.

Fifteen buildings and a few studios now make up the Yaddo complex. But guests still work in solitude, dining on lunch from a tin pail and thermos prepared for them each day. Their work spaces still range from spartan cabins in the woods to rooms filled with elegant furniture from the Trasks' home. Living facilities run the gamut from simple but comfortable garrets and old summer-hotel-style rooms to visions of light and ornament like Katrina Trask's bedroom in the mansion or Main House. "Everyone who's put in there asks if we've made a mistake," Carol Bullard, Yaddo's director of development, says. And nightly meals are eaten in the same large, dark, richly appointed room in which the Trasks dined with their guests.

Beyond that timeless place lies a town that maintains a remarkable balance between the past and present. Commerce in the Trask era is represented in the antique stores found, it seems, on nearly every Saratoga street. But every year new shops spring up to tempt the most discriminating of consumers. Just off Broadway, for instance, Caroline Street is one of Saratoga's livelier small commercial centers. But it is on Phila Street that most of the town's landmark establishments may be found, among them the Lyrical Ballad Bookstore, Caffe Lena, Mrs. London's Bake Shop—whose delicacies were favored by Balanchine—and a town institution called Hattie's Chicken Shack, a tumultuously decorated, serene little neighborhood restaurant known for its home-style Southern cooking and an ambience determined in part by the presence of Bill, the restaurant's elegant host.

Tennis and croquet on the Great Lawn at Yaddo, as photographed in 1884 by Spencer Trask

The Trask family and their guests on the porch at Yaddo in 1887

ABOVE
The future King Victor Emmanuel of Italy with Spencer Trask. Both men are carrying Kodaks, evidently sharing an interest in the new art form.

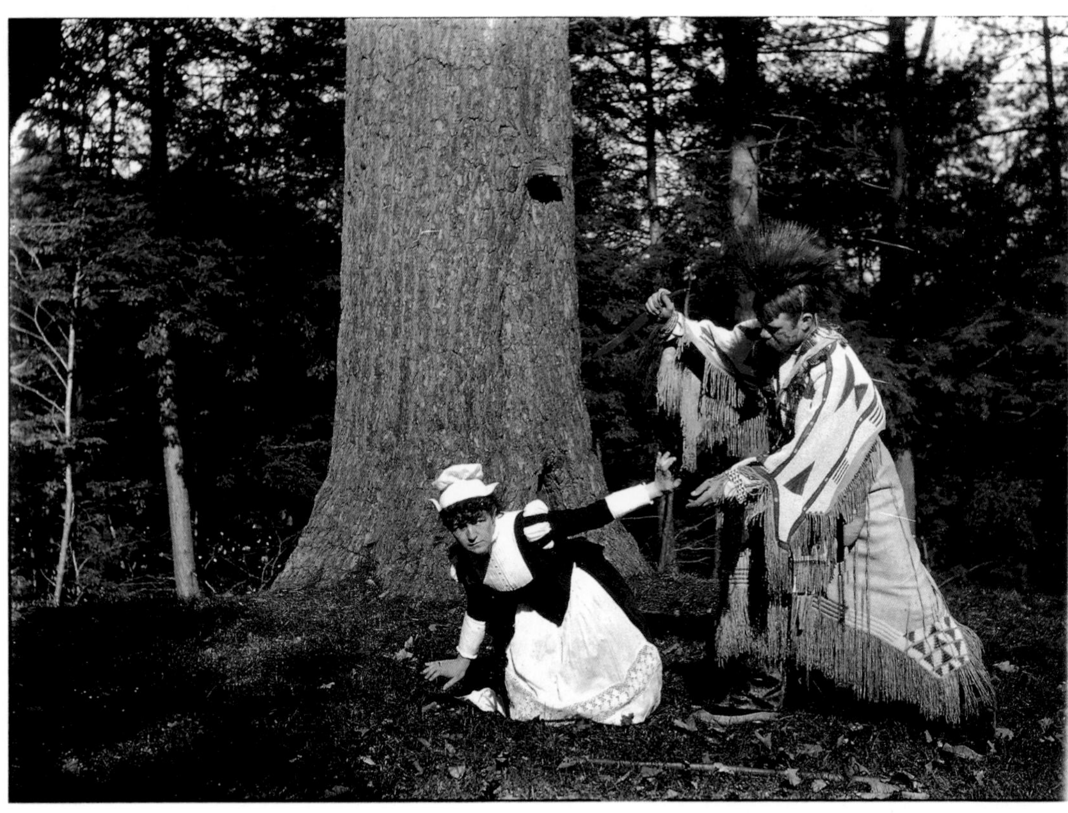

A drama in the woods at Yaddo: Katrina Trask (left) is menaced by a fierce warrior.

Since the Caffe Lena opened in 1960, over five hundred different acts and soloists have appeared on its little stage in a small, comfortable upstairs room. Sipping teas and coffees and eating home-baked pastries, audiences listen to music by the fledgling and the famed. The range of styles is wide, from folk and protest music and black blues to the sounds of jazz and the contemporary women's music movement.

The café can seat from eighty to one hundred, and in the next room there is a fifty-seat theater where innovative drama has been presented by a resident company, visiting actors, and Saratoga's own Home Made Theater. Caffe Lena operates through the year with events at least four times weekly, at prices from $1 to a very rare $15. A gallery was also once part of the café, which is housed in a late-nineteenth-century building that was originally a contractor's offices and woodworking shop.

Like the town library, Caffe Lena is an unofficial community center. Lena Spencer may often be found during concerts seated at the back of the café playing an intent game of Scrabble with her old friend Dorothea Brownell, whom Spencer describes as "a walking encyclopedia of Saratoga lore." But nothing escapes her eagle's eye and ear and accommodating heart. She began with no experience as an impresario and now books entertainers mostly through personal contacts with such musicians as Tom Paxton, Arlo Guthrie, Dave Van Ronk, and David Amram.

Caffe Lena also hosts an "open-mike" night on Thursdays, when a genial, bearded folk musician named Lynn Miller welcomes local and visiting artists and more ordinary mortals to the stage to read poetry, sing, or play a

The Trask children in 1887 with their governess, their ponies, and their dogs

variety of instruments. "We get some young people who are really not ready to perform on stage," Spencer says, "but they never will be if they don't perform." Her latest project is to open the café for afternoon tea. "I have tons of games. People could come watch a soap opera, relax after shopping, study, listen to tapes, or even just talk. Just a place for people to come. They don't even have to buy anything."

That air of cosy accessibility extends to the town's architectural history, too. Saratoga must be one of the few towns in the state where the casual stroller can walk up a main street and find unofficial and official city historians and a library trove of historical books and papers all within a few blocks of each other. But then Saratoga has long been known for its striking nineteenth-century architecture. This city of twenty-five thousand people boasts six National Register Historic Districts, with some nine hundred buildings listed on the National Register of Historic Places, most of them concentrated in the downtown center and immediate residential areas.

Much Saratoga architecture has been destroyed over the years, but in 1977 the citizens of Saratoga decided to fight the deterioration and destruction of its architectural heritage. In that year, the Saratoga Springs Preservation Foundation was formed, and the first historic zoning ordinance was adopted by the city. Through the efforts of the foundation and the city's Historic Review Commission, much of what seemed fated to disappear has, in fact, survived, and the inevitable "development" that any vital community undergoes has been given coherence and coordination. Indeed, a walk in almost any direction from the town's center is likely to take one past architec-

In 1906 a statue was dedicated as a memorial to the Trask children, all of whom had been lost to illness some years before.

Today's Yaddo honors yesterday's intentions by providing its artists-in-residence with a life of insistent grace. Relieved of worldly concerns, writers, painters, and musicians ritually seclude themselves from breakfast to dinner. Flowers from the gardens laid out by Katrina and Spencer Trask adorn the un-common spaces where creativity can only be discussed after 5 P.M.

tural wonders. And walks along Franklin Square and Franklin Street, North Broadway, Union Avenue, and Circular Street are rewarding treasure hunts.

The most lavish of those treasures is the Batcheller Mansion at 20 Circular Street, a magnificent efflorescence of the High Victorian Mansard or French Renaissance style of mid-nineteenth-century Saratoga architecture. Henry James might have had buildings like this in mind when he described Saratoga as "ostentatious." But the mansion's profusion of towers, chimneys, and ornate turrets and its jumbled porches, balconies, and balustrades have an infectious exuberance that masks an underlying architectural order. This is Victorian embellishment and Saratoga eclecticism at their most affecting.

The mansion was designed by Nichols and Halcott of Albany and built in 1873 for George Sherman Batcheller, who in 1875 was appointed by President Grant to the International Tribunal of Egypt. The steep-sloping windowed mansard roofs characteristic of the French Renaissance architectural style are modified here. But the house has the kind of large-scale and complex, irregular facade and ornamentation that is not only peculiar to the style but proclaims the owner's wealth and success.

A sense of what the interior looked like a century or so ago may be had with a visit to the colorful and atmospheric Museum of the Historical Society of Saratoga Springs, which is housed in the Casino in Congress Park, at the center of town. The affectionate town pride that makes the museum so welcoming is also to be found in the Phila Street shop of George Bolster, a genial unofficial town historian whose hand-tinted photographs of old Saratoga pro-

A stained-glass tribute to the waters of Saratoga Springs, a statue to the muses, and lunch buckets to sustain the artists in their seclusion convey silent messages in Yaddo's halls.

vide another useful departure point for a tour of Saratoga architecture.

The soft curves and edgily intersecting lines of the expansive white house at 104 Union Avenue make it a perfect example of architecture as physicalized music. But this is also an example of the mid-nineteenth-century High Victorian Italianate or Lombardian style in Saratoga, with its low roofs and overhanging eaves with decorative brackets, its round-arched windows with wood moldings, and its balustraded balconies and porches. Note, here, the addition of the curved Queen Anne porch in typically eclectic Saratoga style.

To walk through Franklin Square and Franklin Street, facing west from the humming commerce of low-lying Broadway, is to feel as if one has wandered into another era. In this architectural enclave may be found several early Saratoga buildings. Houses at 59 and 63 Franklin Street are particularly pure examples of the Greek Revival style of the early and mid-nineteenth century, notable for its bare geometric regularity, its flat white-painted wooden facade, and its forthright columns, pilasters, and simple moldings. If the Batcheller Mansion proclaimed achievement, these rectangular houses, severely symmetrical, proclaimed their owners' rectitude. These were clearly "wooden temples to house a new race of democrats," as Joan C. Siegfried puts it in *The Nineteenth Century Architecture of Saratoga.*

Of the beautiful, sprawling homes on North Broadway that were built by wealthy summer visitors, two repay close scrutiny. Number 722, also known as Kilmer House, is in the Late Victorian Queen Anne style of the final

Caffé Lena
SARATOGA STRING SHOP
CAFFE LENA
Skidmore College
Lena Rose Spencer
Doctor of Humane Letters
CAFFE LENA
Priscilla Herdman
"One of the clearest and most compelling voices of contemporary folk music." The New York Times
Saturday Sept. 12 8:30 p.m.
47 Phila Street • Saratoga Springs, New York
CAFFE LENA
TOM CHAPIN

years of the nineteenth century, with its contrasting stone ground story and shingled upper floors, its steep roofs and tall chimneys and patterns of repeated windows. Chockablock with towers and gables, its upper surface a compendium of shingle patterns, the house is a symphony of slate—blue and darker grays that are brought out in a touch of purple in lovely grape-colored stained-glass panels that the eye discerns only with difficulty. Note, too, the tracery of the gable apexes in 754 North Broadway, whose elaborately decorative nature places them in the Late Victorian Gothic style.

Lena Spencer was granted an honorary Doctorate of Humane Letters by Skidmore College for pioneering her folk-music coffeehouse.

One finds gazebos of every degree of complexity and imagination tucked into the wide green lawns of this serenely affluent neighborhood. An outstanding example may be found blooming from the bushes and trees at the back of 760 North Broadway, a sample at once severe and frivolous of Post-Victorian Colonial Revival style. Like an outcropping of chalk cliff in all that greenery, the home itself is of no special architectural note, but its easy blend of plainness and ornament seems typical of the Saratoga spirit.

And solid commercial values are reflected unabashedly in the imposing brick Italian palazzo-style City Hall on Broadway and the block of brick buildings at the southeast corner of Broadway and Lake Avenue. The more recently erected Ramada Renaissance Hotel and Saratoga Springs City Center building to the north appears to be an ugly and misguided attempt to blend in with the red-brick facades of this main commercial thoroughfare.

A walk around the area of Regent, Caroline, and Phila streets yields a taste of another kind of life. There are architectural gems here, too, among them 198 Regent Street, a sweet little pink wooden cottage in Greek Revival style—once owned by City Ballet principal dancer Patricia McBride—as well as a richly detailed green-and-cream-painted brick home at 150 Phila Street, another good example of the High Victorian Mansard style, and the delicately and imaginatively decorated gray-and-white wooden home in Victorian Gothic style at 184 Phila Street. And for an idea of the sad architectural neglect once prevalent in Saratoga, there is the battered but still handsomely mansarded ghost of an abandoned building on the southeast corner of Caroline and Regent streets.

All that remains of the great hotels for which the town was famous are the Adelphi and the Rip Van Dam on Broadway, originally lower- and middle-class family hotels, whose long, high front porches represent a distinctive feature of Saratoga architecture. The Rip, as it is popularly known, was once the American Hotel and was renamed for the first owner of the land on which Saratoga's High Rock spring was discovered.

Like Topsy, the Rip just grew and grew. Its south wing was built in 1819 and the main hotel in 1840, with two motels added at the back in the 1960s. Its guests tend to be repeaters, asking for the same room season after season. For example, when Sophie Pourmel, City Ballet's wardrobe mistress, retired, her regular room was taken over by Leslie "Ducky" Copeland, the company's male-wardrobe supervisor.

The Rip has the spare, friendly ambience of a large Scottish bed-and-breakfast. The Adelphi, originally built in 1877 on the site of the Old Adelphia Hotel, is a dizzying but beautiful tumble into High Victoriana, newly

renovated by Sheila Parkert and Gregg Siefker. Having fallen in love with the town and the City Ballet during a college camping trip, the two returned to open a small grocery, then take over a restaurant, and finally acquire the hotel on a shoestring in 1983.

Saratoga is a town constantly sprucing itself up. On warm days, the sounds of buzz saws, hammers, and lawn mowers are everywhere in the distant air. But there are few renovation stories like the Adelphi. "We always had our eye on this," Parkert says. "But we didn't have any money, and it was a horrible wreck." With some initial help from investors, the two took over the abandoned and vandalized hotel and began to work on it room by room. First, they fixed up and opened the handsome bar, a dancers' hangout from the start. Today, twenty-eight of the hotel's thirty-eight rooms are finished.

Parkert did extensive historical research on design, and the hotel has been furnished almost exclusively with furniture and artifacts in period styles from the 1830s to the 1920s, most of them found at flea markets, garage sales, and auctions in the area. Parkert sewed the curtains. Siefker and Bob Wheaton, a local friend and artisan, did everything from stenciling ceilings and plastering walls to plumbing and wiring, with very little outside help. "The first time you pay a plumber, you realize you've got to start learning," Siefker says.

There seems to have been very little tradition of concert dance in Saratoga before SPAC. Mention is made in an 1871 issue of *The Saratogian* newspaper that a "Mr. Loomis, of Springfield, Mass., trod the floor gracefully

Breakfast on the piazza (left), one story above Broadway, brings a family back into the 1870s, when the Adelphi Hotel and its neighbor, the Rip Van Dam (above), were also young.

FOLLOWING PAGES

The time warp continues as one encounters Congress Park, with Bertel Thorvaldsen's monumental urn honoring motherhood framing Canfield's Casino (pp. 114–115). On Broadway (pp. 116–117), the explosive growth of 1871 is still witnessed by the City Hall (with flags) and the Italianate office block (with bunting). Victorian masons took time to grace Saratoga with rich texture (pp. 118–119).

The National Register of Historic Places lists no less than six "Historic Districts" within the Saratoga Springs Urban Cultural Park. Whether it be a turreted Tudor rooming house in the Union Avenue District or John Morrissey's 1867 Italianate gambling casino in the Congress Park District, Saratoga's vintage buildings are now seen as landmarks of unusual historic and aesthetic interest. Saratoga's patch-up-and-paint season is year-round.

in the guise of a Ballet Dancer" in a "Grand Masquerade" at the Congress Hall. But if a good deal of Saratoga's economic rise a century later has to do with SPAC, and the most distinctive season in the summer-long festival is presented by City Ballet, then it is not surprising that the dancers seem, in turn, to have made strong and important ties with the community of Saratoga.

Michael Steele danced for eleven years with City Ballet, which he left in 1973. "When Balanchine told us about our new summer home, I had only heard of Sarasota," Steele recalls. Today he lives on a sheep ranch outside Saratoga. He also owns real estate and runs Ballet Regent, a prominent Saratoga ballet school he established with his partner, Tomislav Vukovich.

Steele's first summer in town, he rented a room from a kindly Italian family who kept telling him, "Take it easy, Mike." He made friends the first year and, by the company's third season, had acquired a charming old cottage in the heart of town. "Saratoga was this wonderful, sleepy little town to retire to," Steele remembers. "Mr. Balanchine and all of us loved coming here. It was like a vacation, except we all worked even harder, if anything, because it was so lovely here and there was such a nice atmosphere. The first year, we often felt there were more of us on stage than in the audience. Now the whole town hums, 'The ballet is coming, the ballet is coming.' You can feel the atmosphere change. Everyone loves the dancers. In August, people are making money. In July, it's just the festivity."

Shopkeepers are more blasé now about the ballet, no longer offering eager opinions on the dancing of such performers as "Melinda" Hayden. Today, the City Ballet no longer has to import its child dancers from New

York City, though Steele groans over the uphill struggle he waged in establishing a ballet school in the town. There are other differences. "SPAC was the shot in the arm that I think put Saratoga back on the map," Steele says. "It was almost like a ghost town when SPAC opened. Every other house was boarded up. But Saratoga has changed a great deal." His own love for the town led him to learn its history and explore its beauties early in the City Ballet's summer tenancy. The first dancer to buy here, he helped others to locate special and affordable homes in the area. "In 1966, you could buy almost any house in town for ten thousand dollars. Now you can't buy anything halfway decent for under a hundred-and-something thousand. But I'm just really glad Saratoga is experiencing a renaissance and going in a good direction."

As he talks, Saratoga is winding back to its normal pace. It is early September and the streets are quieter now. A salesclerk at Woolworth's looks up from her customer for a moment as a police car passes, siren wailing. "Something must be happening," she says mildly. Saratogians have returned to homes rented out in August. A fugitive, spicy scent of petunias still fills the air in this town of gaily filled window boxes and neat public flower beds. But out at SPAC, wind whips flag ropes against their poles and cawing crows have the festival grounds to themselves. A young mother wheels her baby into the nearby Hall of Springs, on her way to pick up the last paycheck of the summer. The Hall's summer dinners are ended. Its exquisite banquet chamber is empty. But in the festival offices upstairs, there is busy negotiation of the dreams and details of seasons to come in Saratoga.

THIS PAGE AND OPPOSITE
Saratoga's architectural flagship is the 1873 Batcheller Mansion at 20 Circular Street.

FOLLOWING PAGES
Its visual poetry, embellished with hyperbole, contrast, and analogy, conveys the Victorian vision of a French Renaissance château, crowned by a Moorish Revival minaret. With mansard-inspired rooflines, embellished chimney pots, alliterating arches, and Venetian balconies, this eclectic gem offers splendid testament to yesterday's construction skills and today's drive to restore. Fifteen years ago, the Batcheller Mansion was described as "vandalized and in disrepair."

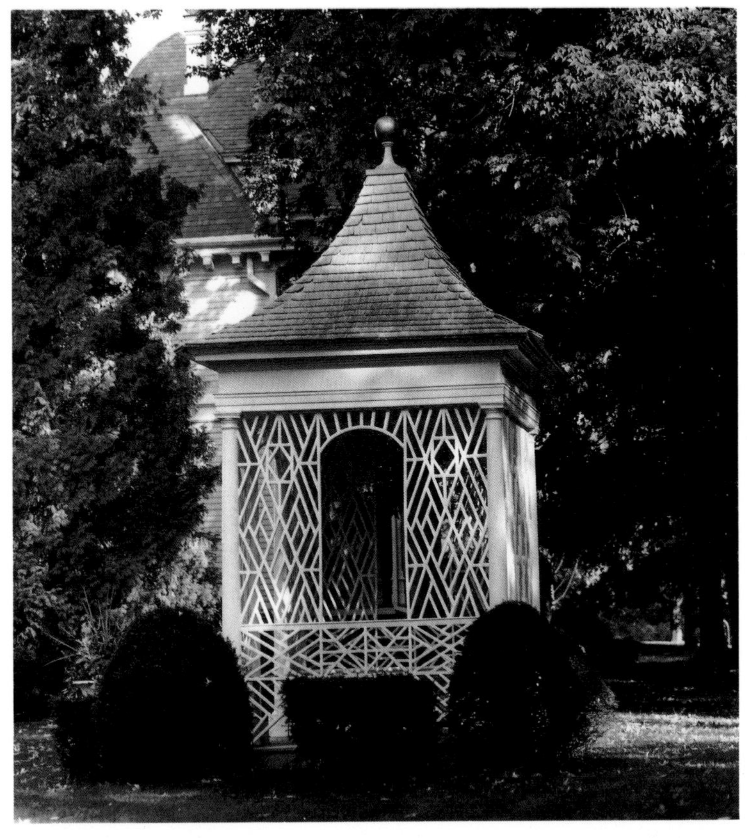

As resorts offer retreat from an urban world, so vacationers enjoy respite from the promenading and partying of resort life. A Doric-columned porch cupola at 102 Union Avenue (left) and Chinese Chippendale (top) and Colonial Revival (bottom) gazebos behind North Broadway manses are vintage rest stops in which to slow the merry pace and let the soul catch up with the body.

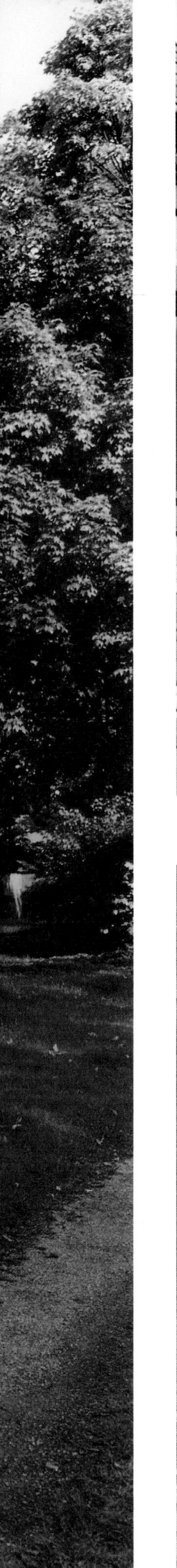

With a varied roofline expressing the ideals of High Victorian Gothic, and a rough-hewn stone porch and variegated shingles in the Queen Anne manner, the Kilmer House at 722 North Broadway offers delight for passersby and cozy nooks for residents.

The High Victorian Gothic gables at 754 North Broadway (left) have apexes embellished in the Ornamental Villa manner, while the neighboring home of the same period (right) borrows its apex adornment from the later Stick style.

The mansard roofline at 150 Phila Street caps a tiered cake embellished with gables, cornices, arches, and dormers. Aluminum storm windows and porch screening convey the imperatives of modern comfort.

Arch upon arch, arch within arch, 184 Phila Street—under restoration—aspires to the heavens while it greets visitors with engraved glass portals.

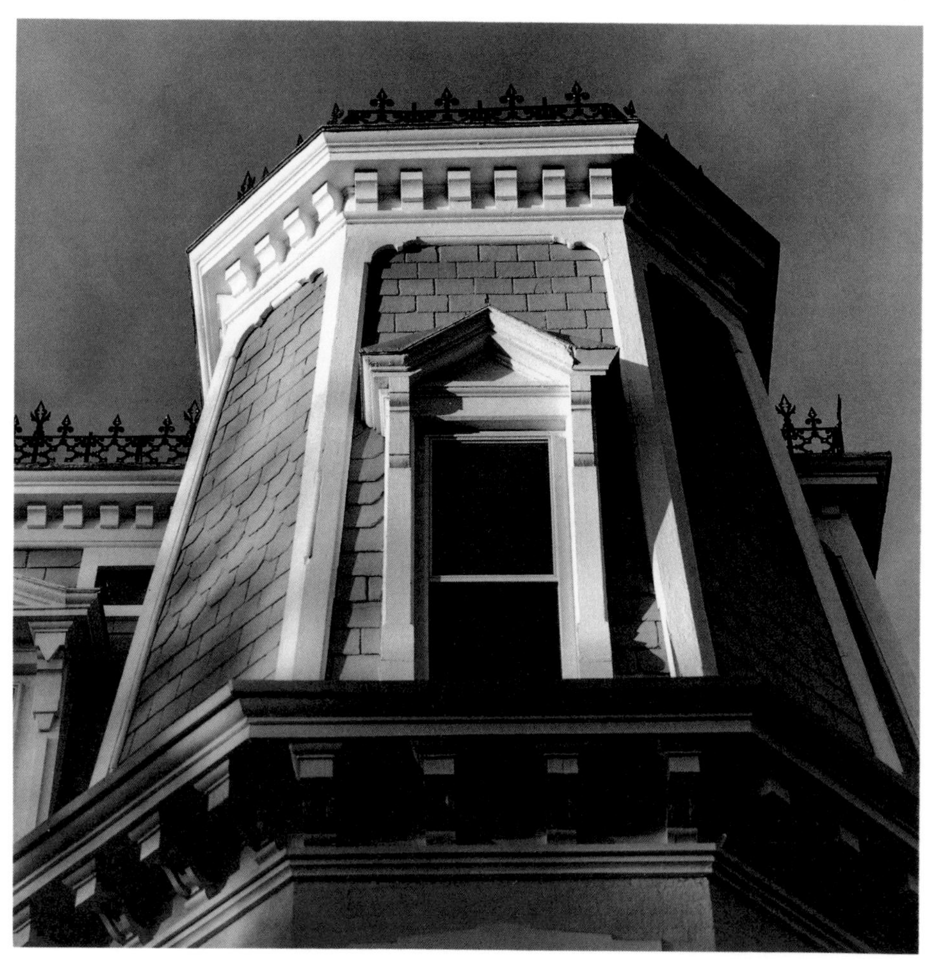

On Caroline Street there is ample evidence of the bright future and troubled past of Saratoga's Victorian heritage.

Man o' War

Chapter III

RACING AND THE SOCIAL LIFE

by Whitney Tower

The Office of this paper is removed to
102 CHAMBERS STREET,
or. Church, one block from Broadway. Address as heretofore, P. O. Box 938.
THIRTY-TWO PAGES
SPIRIT OF THE TIMES
"THE SPIRIT OF THE TIMES SHALL TEACH ME SPEED"
King John Act IV.

A Chronicle of the Turf, Field Sports, Aquatics, Agriculture, and the Stage.

VOL. 94—No. 8.
No. 102 CHAMBERS STREET

NEW YORK, SATURDAY, SEPTEMBER 29, 1877.

SUBSCRIPTION:
FIVE DOLLARS A YEAR

2:23 SMALL HOPES AND LADY MAC. 2:23

Mr. W. H. Vanderbilt's Celebrated Road Team.

We present to our readers this week a spirited sketch of Mr. Wm. H. Vanderbilt and his grand pair of trotters, Small Hopes and Lady Mac, which, on the 11th of the present month, made the circuit of Fleetwood Park in the unparalleled time of 2:23. Although not a technical record, the performance created as much enthusiasm throughout the land as if the time had been made in a race for money against other horses, and this feeling was, doubtless, enhanced by the fact that the wealthiest man in the country held the ribbons over the flyers. We are confident that we gratify a general curiosity when we present this picture, and can assure our readers that it contains portraits of the three principal actors. It is, in fact, a representation of a great many millions of dollars driving a great many thousands of dollars worth of horse-flesh, a spectacle which may be frequently seen, though rarely to this extent, on the favorite drives about our large cities, especially those of New York, but one of which our country readers will take particular pleasure in witnessing the delineation. In our issue succeeding the performance which this picture commemorates, we gave a very full account of it, and it is sufficient, as a matter of record, to recapitulate here that, on the 11th inst., after the colt race for THE SPIRIT OF THE TIMES Stakes had been finished at Fleetwood Park, Mr. Vanderbilt came on the track in a road wagon, weighing with himself, 346½ pounds, drawn by Small Hopes and Lady Mac, and requested the judges, who were still in the stand, to take the time of the team for a brush around the track. They assented, and, after a little warming up, they came flying down to the score, and trotted the entire mile without a break, going to the quarter pole in 34½s., pass the half in 1:10½, the three-quarter pole in 1:46½, and completing the mile in precisely 2:23. The excellence of this performance can be best appreciated when we state that the fastest double-team time of record, previously, was 2:26½, made by Gen. Cobb and Lulu May, at San Francisco, Cal., last June, and the fastest authenticated double-team time, not a record, was 2:25¼, which stands to the credit of Mr. Joseph Harker's team, Bruno and Brunette, the performance having been made to road wagon, in 1867. Another very notable double-team performance was that of Mr. Robert Bonner's Lady Palmer and Flatbush Maid, driven by himself, in 1862, the time being 2:26. By way of explanation of our present picture, we will say that the off-horse, the one of which a full side-view is presented, is Lady Mac, while the trotter, partially hid, with the white hind feet, is Small Hopes. Mr. Forbes has succeeded in producing the most life-like picture of a pair of trotters at full speed that we have ever seen, and the point of view selected has been chosen with an artist's eye. A different view might have better displayed the unity of the motion of the team, but would have been much less spirited, and not afforded so good an opportunity for a portrait of the millionaire driver, and his style of holding the lines. In connection with the affair, the following letter from Wm. McGuigan, the man who drove the most celebrated of the equine performers in Mr. Vanderbilt's fast ride, Small Hopes, throughout his notorious campaign of 1875, will be read with great interest:

"Having noticed, in your last issue, the great performance of my little brown favorite, Small Hopes, with his aliases, you will, I hope, grant me space to give vent to my feelings concerning him, as I never can in the least tire of talking or writing of him. It is not possible for any man on earth to have the least idea how much confidence I have in his ability to trot faster than any horse that ever lived, for one or two miles. You call the team 'incomparable.' I have, a long time ago, called him the 'incomparable trotter,' and the only word fit to describe his gait is *perfection*. Two years ago, when I trotted him here and allowed him to be beaten, he could, in the last heat, not only have beaten White Stockings, but I am confident he could have beaten any other horse, and, at Omaha, the next week, he could have beaten 2:20 over that half-mile and seventeen feet too long track, as sure as two and two are four. I have, in previous letters, stated my confidence in this horse, but was laughed at. I wrote to Dan Mace, a short time before Mr. Vanderbilt bought him, telling him to come and buy him, as he would have no trouble in getting him reinstated, and that he could beat every horse living over any track in the United States; that it mattered not, mud, sand, or a hard track, he could win, as I had tried him over them all under the most severe and trying circumstances that ever a horse was tried, and that, at Washington, in the eleventh heat, within two days, he had more speed at the finish than any horse ever had at the last of a mile. To take all things into consideration he was the greatest of all trotters, living or dead. I got no answer from Dan, but I notice he now says he can drive him and mate better than 2:20, and, no doubt, he can, for I know 2:20 is mere play for Small Hopes on any good mile track. I would willingly this day, if he was as he was at this place the last day, at Omaha, or at Washington the last days and heats, allow a thousand soldiers to stand with loaded guns, with orders to shoot me through if I did not beat 2:14, were it over Mystic, Kalamazoo, Freeport, or Saginaw tracks, and them in as good condition as I have seen either of them; my confidence in his beating 2:14 would be so great that it would be impossible for him to fail any more than it would for him to fail to beat 2:40. My great desire is yet to show to a doubting public that he is all and more than I ever claimed him to be. Many, in reading what Dan Mace and others say regarding a team trotting as fast double as single, are mistaken, either because they do not understand Mr. Mace or because Dan has made a wrong statement, for, allow me to say here, there never was a team so evenly matched that it could beat 2:30 together, but that I could take my choice of them and beat their time double, with Mr. Mace or any other man behind them. While it may be that Dan can take Small Hopes and Lady Mac and trot a mile faster than Lady Mac can trot single, it is not true of the other. If it was possible for any practical horseman to know what I know about Small Hopes' ability to trot fast and keep up his clip to the end of a mile, they would say, as I do, 2:14 would be beaten as sure as ever he undertook to beat it under favorable circumstances. Is not Mr. Vanderbilt a man of fortune and good luck? To think that, for a few thousand dollars, and the gift of a father, he has a faster single or double horse than all the wealth in the world can buy! Yours, WM. MCGUIGAN, JR."

"They are all well-dressed, this Saratoga racing crowd. There is no place here for the tin-horn gambler, and the poorest of the lot could doubtless dig down into his trousers pocket and produce a roll, which in the picturesque parlance of the ring, 'would choke a cow.'"

Louis McHenry Howe, "Saratoga Springs," *New England Magazine,* Vol. XXXII

Among the world's racetracks there is nothing comparable to Saratoga, with the backstretch of its main track, the old and new stables across Union Avenue at Horse Haven, and the Oklahoma training-track facilities, where in 1863 Thoroughbred racing first took hold here. The soft mist rises slowly over the straight, stately trees and over the ancient barns adjacent to the creaking stands that have looked down upon the exploits of Man o' War and Secretariat and hundreds of thousands of lesser runners over the course of one hundred twenty-five years. There is the sound of hoofbeats, the chatter in mixed languages and accents of a cast of thousands—jockeys, grooms, exercise help; the filling of feed tubs at the barns where the smell of horses, their entourage, and equipment mingles with the aroma of breakfasts being dished up on the Clubhouse terrace to the accompaniment of clinking glasses of juice and, naturally, here and there the glass of something stronger, which is a carry-over from the days when the breakfast crowd appeared in evening dresses and tuxedos and Bollinger champagne was more familiar than juice.

The flavor of the place, if you are on track grounds, hasn't changed all that much, and there remains a sort of common ground for anyone who is drawn to Saratoga these days—nostalgia, perhaps, for a gentler time. The wooden stands with their Victorian spires are a country fair. The quality of horses and competition—owners continue to bring their best horses—bespeak solid professionalism. I may be naive or sentimental, but I believe that most Saratoga racegoers are in that rickety old stand, mornings and afternoons, because they like the racing and they like the atmosphere of both Saratogas, track and town.

PRECEDING PAGES
Racing mementos from Man o' War's career, which began at Saratoga's yearling sales, suggest the richness of the National Museum of Racing's collection and the sense of history-in-the-making that pervades the August season at America's oldest track.

OPPOSITE
William H. Vanderbilt, in his day perhaps the richest man in America, personified the best of the sporting society that frequented Saratoga: a multimillionaire railroad tycoon who could drive a world-class pair of trotters to high performance.

Before the days of track-controlled pari-mutuel betting, bookmakers belonging to the Metropolitan Turf Association accommodated private wagers and offered auction pools to the racetrack's sporting set. Today's New York Racing Association profits make a significant contribution to the state's educational funds.

What was once a sparkling little town that burst its seams for four fat weeks in August has become a thriving city, which, regardless of what visitors might have thought in the past, has far more going for it than its racetrack, the oldest active one in the United States. New people have come to town, either to do business or to live out their retirement years, and many residents commute to work in the larger cities of the Capital Area. They have joined with other locals in supporting the Saratoga Performing Arts Center; they are proud when an alumnus of the Yaddo artist colony is acclaimed; and they are honored that the new National Museum of Dance chose Saratoga as its permanent home.

But above all else, they look to Skidmore College, for so long thought of as a so-so all-female institution, now entirely remade largely through the efforts of its president, the late Joseph C. Palamountain, Jr., and his wife, Anne. Today, Skidmore occupies an entirely new 1,200–acre campus with a co-ed student body of over 2,000. Once located in the middle of downtown, it now sits but a couple of chip shots away from stylish North Broadway, that elm- and maple-lined boulevard along which, over the years, sprang up a mixed bag of mansions and sprawling lawns. Many of the houses were built between 1895 and World War I, and no two are the same. Skidmore's president's house, for example, is a circa-1902 design of pure Colonial Revival aspirations. Others follow Victorian Gothic or Queen Anne or Greek Revival lines, while here and there one finds a touch of Baroque, Italian villa, or French château. Eclectic is the word.

North Broadway's "cottages" have always been known for their plethora of porches and mishmashes of porticoes, cupolas, pillars, balconies, turrets, towers, and bays. There is a little something for everybody, which on North Broadway is to say something for such familiar racing names as Jeffords, Phipps, Galbreath, Farish, Brady, Gaines, and lately, Brant. On the southern end of this establishment neighborhood is the house of Mollie Wilmot. Party-giving Mollie is heavily into racing, too, but probably she is better known as the Palm Beach beach-fronter who woke one morning to find the freighter *Mercedes* parked in her swimming pool. The uninvited guest stayed for one hundred days!

The rest of Saratoga, with the exception of the parts of Union Avenue once occupied by Skidmore—and now surrounding the new digs of the city's second undergraduate school, Empire State College—little resembles North Broadway. But neither do many of the city streets duplicate the eyesore of South Broadway and its collection of auto showrooms, motels, and fast-food outlets.

Congress Park, at the foot of Union Avenue and just off downtown Broadway, with the old Canfield Casino front and center, is as lovely as ever. Up Union is the track itself, a majestic exception to the concrete-and-glass horrors that have sprung up elsewhere. The elm-studded paddock area and new picnic grounds gracefully accommodate today's larger-than-ever crowds. Across Union is the National Museum of Racing and Hall of Fame, built in 1955 and now undergoing a $6 million interior refurbishing at the hands of a team of English museum specialists—with a gala reopening planned for 1988.

Everywhere one looks in Saratoga there are signs of vitality, a commodity in low supply during the 1950s when the nightclubs went out of business and the track's attendance and pari-mutuel handle shrunk. Salvation, ultimately, came through the good offices of men like John W. Hanes, Captain Harry F. Guggenheim, and Christopher T. Chenery, who incorporated racing in Saratoga with racing at the Belmont and Aqueduct tracks, thereby most likely saving the sport at all three places.

The formation of the nonprofit New York Racing Association (NYRA) brought all three of the state's tracks under control of one body of trustees—all of whom originally came from the ranks of The Jockey Club—and they made it their primary business to consolidate the financial affairs of the three enterprises. Through a synchronized stakes program and coordinated publicity and advertising campaigns, they saw New York racing embark on an effort to regain its lost prestige as well as the number-one position in Thoroughbred sport.

Since its inception in 1955, according to statistics provided by *The Blood-Horse* magazine, NYRA has paid more than $1.8 billion to New York State in pari-mutuel-related revenue. In 1986 alone, $59,600,000 in revenue was generated by NYRA for distribution among four state agencies: the New York State Tax Commission, the New York State Racing and Wagering Board, the New York Thoroughbred Breeding and Development Fund, and the New York State Capital Investment Fund. In addition, NYRA contributed

Winslow Homer's eye caught the spirited 1865 season at the newly opened racetrack at Saratoga. With the Civil War just over and America's great period of industrial expansion about to begin, Saratoga entered its heyday as a sporting and courting capital.

FOLLOWING PAGES
By the early 20th century a cartoon saw Saratoga as the Monte Carlo of America, which indeed it was.

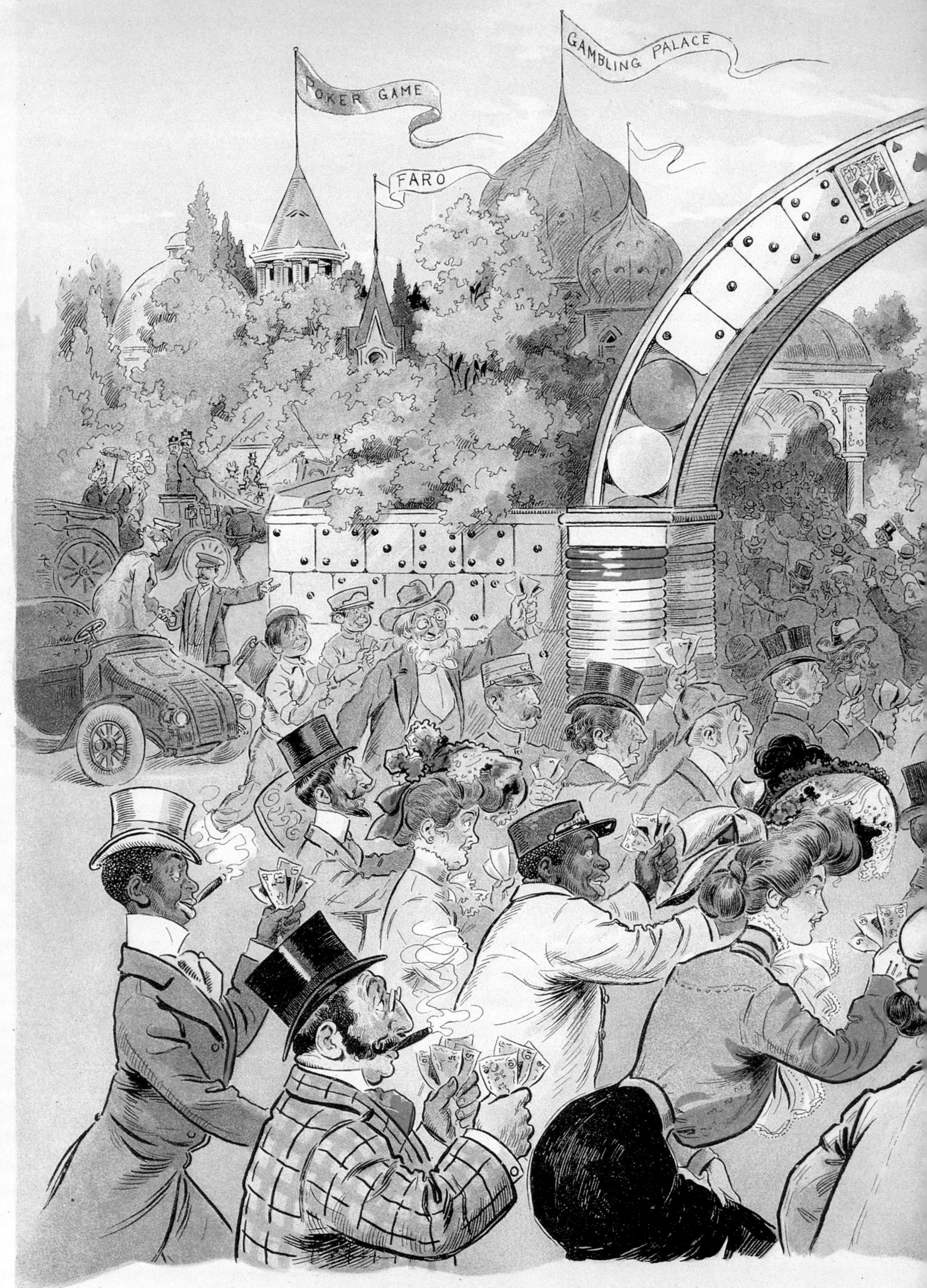

J. OTTMANN LITH. CO. PUCK BLDG. N.Y.

ONCE MORE HI

UNCLE SAM.—Biggest trade, biggest trusts, biggest buildings, b

EADS THE WORLD.

nachinery, and now I 've got the biggest gambling joint. Well, say!

WELCOME
NEW
SKIDMORE
STUDENTS
WELCOME
NEW
SKIDMORE
STUDENTS
WELCOME
NEW
SKIDMORE
STUDENTS

approximately $11 million in real estate taxes to local governments in 1986.

For all the efforts of businessmen and goodwill organizations, every community's crucial move upward is usually the handiwork of one ringleader. In Saratoga, that honor belongs to Mrs. Cornelius Vanderbilt Whitney, or for short, Marylou. Never mind that she gets her picture and her opinions in the local papers every day, or that her Clubhouse box at the track is a bottleneck of television cameras and their endlessly twisting cables. Mind only that Marylou Whitney, married to the grandson of William C.—who, generations back, was largely responsible for "cleaning up" the track by buying out or overruling most of the presiding undesirables—is one of the big wheels who make modern Saratoga click, especially in the summer season.

"She is not only a celebrity," says one Saratogian, "she is *our* celebrity. She could run for any office in Saratoga and win in a landslide." Marylou, Pat Linden once wrote in *Town & Country*, is "nip-waisted, leghorn-hatted and ruffly as all get-out, Marylou's porcelain-skinned, belle-of-Tara look is a foil for her stalwart and generous soul. A relentless hostess, fundraiser and benefactor and publicist, she is the stage mother who keeps Saratoga on its social and promotional toes."

The description is apt. One of the reasons Saratoga works so well, or seems to for the majority of Saratogians and for those they refer to as the "summer" or the "August" people, is that Marylou is the master of the social mix. She and her press agent friends can be excused her gaffe a few years back when she said that nothing had ever happened in Saratoga before she got there. She more than compensated by launching a series of parties aimed at touching all bases of every social stratum, and if you aren't invited to one dinner-and-movie soiree in the pool house, you may get the nod to the next garden party.

The lady once regarded by some people as an intruder—she had come from the Midwest—is cheered heartily for her charitable work. She is cheered, too, for the royal manner she adopts at her annual bash at the Canfield Casino, but in the words of one townsman, "This is a good example of a love-hate relationship." Marylou usually arrives at her by-invitation-only affair in a carriage and greets her celebrated guests with delicate, Queen Mum–like waves, most of them aimed at a crowd of hundreds huddled by the Casino entrance. This is where the democracy of the garden parties gives way to the exclusivity of a soiree in a palace ballroom. "The locals love to hate her or, more correctly, to hate the life and wealth she represents," says the observer. "But they love to cheer her, too. They'll stand all night in the rain just to see her celebrity friends going into a party they will never receive an invitation to."

They know they are going to see Marylou houseguests like Esther Williams, Kirk Douglas, Ginger Rogers, and Walter Cronkite, but they know that long after those people have left town, Marylou will be around doing remarkable things, such as showing up at the Marylou look-alike contest at Siro's restaurant. While several hundred contestants, including a few males, were being judged, Marylou popped in unexpectedly not only to assist in the judging but also to mix it up for an hour or so with the would-be look-alikes.

A Skidmore student's season spans four years of education, both on and off campus. International resort by summer, county seat and college town by winter, Saratoga is one of America's biggest small towns.

First light begins the backstretch day at the Oklahoma training track, itself as old as racing at Saratoga. In use from spring to winter for schooling, the grounds accommodate 1,700 Thoroughbreds during the August racing season.

FOLLOWING PAGES

A morning's workout (pp. 152–153) can be a few halter-led laps for a two-year-old or a fast six furlongs for a three-year-old being prepared for a race. At the main track stables (pp. 154–155), the hot-walkers and grooms take over from the exercise riders, cooling down and washing, then brushing and feeding the nobility of the horse world. And they hope, as they clean the tack (pp. 156–157), that their morning's charge will be, like Forego, another "Hall of Famer" at the National Museum of Racing.

This is not to say that other hostesses in Saratoga are not pulling their oars. Kay Jeffords has such delicious and full prerace luncheons that upon reaching the Clubhouse boxes one wishes the seats were reclining chaises. And an evening at Mollie Wilmot's, be it to tear at some Colonel Sanders chicken limbs on the porch or to wind up a 3 A.M. late-nighter dancing to a Neal Smith combo, is a treat to be savored.

Equally to be relished—no, to be thankful for, at least for those who return to Saratoga summer after summer—is the inherited energy that carried their great-grandparents through the same drill one hundred years ago. Certainly the old energy still survives, though it sometimes flags. Even armed with superhuman stamina, one caught in the rounds of Saratoga socializing can find it exhausting. A few years ago a young man I know managed only ten days as a Saratoga houseguest. At the end he checked himself into the Saratoga Hospital for four days of "freshening up" before he dared show himself at home.

Money, to be sure, rolls into Saratoga by the vault load each midsummer. And, as is the custom in summer resorts everywhere, the local merchants are not going to be holding the short end of the stick come Labor Day. Prices climb, especially for hotel rooms, the most expensive costing as much as $410 for an ordinary double and $700 for a suite. Comfortable houses that rented for $800 or $1,000 in the late sixties are $10,000 and up today.

Back in what we now cheerfully refer to as "the old days," people rented houses cheaply or stayed in leviathan hotels like the United States or Grand Union. They guzzled champagne at such nightclubs as Arrowhead, Piping Rock, or Brook, listened to the humor of Joe E. Lewis, the songs of Sophie Tucker and Helen Morgan, and they danced to the rhythmic music of old smoothies like Vincent Lopez and Ben Bernie. The tunes of Victor Herbert and John Philip Sousa and the voices of Enrico Caruso and Ernestine Schumann-Heink, heard even earlier, have been replaced by symphonies and ballets at the Saratoga Performing Arts Center.

Then as now the late-stayers managed to get to the track for breakfast. They watched the morning workouts and began figuring out exactly how best to deploy their daily quotient of energy in the ensuing twenty-four hours. The gambling, thanks to Senator Estes Kefauver and Governor Thomas E. Dewey, has gone the way of the walking stick and spats, but nights once spent at the illegal gaming tables now are more leisurely passed at private dinners or in public eateries, where the chances of being interrupted by the wail of a police siren are but two: slim or none.

One has always had a great need in Saratoga for a well-tuned liver. I like to think that in my grandfather's time—and in his father's day before him—the racing community managed to balance their dining and other pleasures decorously with their civic obligations. I would hate to think that yesterday's gentry faced the daunting mornings so common today, when one picks up one's *Daily Racing Form* only to be startlingly reminded morning after morning that half of every day must be spent in meetings and half of every evening at "must" charity functions. A losing all-night poker game at the turn of the century had to be easier on one's system.

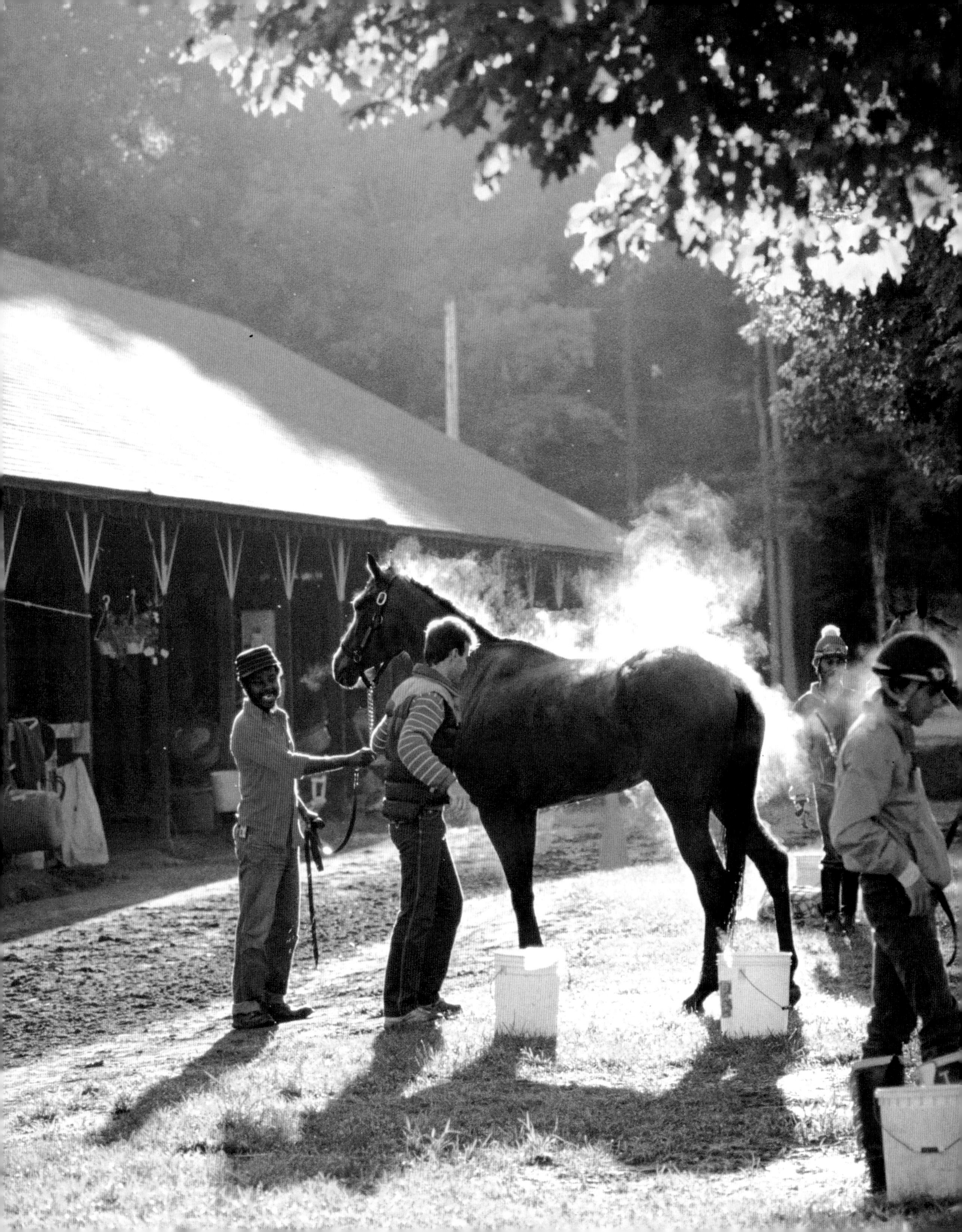

FOREGO

As Nicholas Brady remarks: "Coming to Saratoga is a time-honored tradition. You're able to get close to your horses. You literally can be out at the track at 6 A.M. and be involved in the training and planning that Thoroughbred racing is all about. All that by 9, and then back to the house for breakfast with friends.... There have been some unbelievable conversations on this porch. My father used to love to sit here and talk. There have been some interesting plans hatched right here. You can get to the heart of it—the sales, the racing, the breeding plans. Racing is a game of futures, and the future *starts right here."*

153 4000000

A bet on the future doesn't come cheap at the Fasig-Tipton yearling sales. Inevitably, high wagers on horses like "153" are based on stakes-winning performances in the bloodlines. A Danzig filly, "121" is a granddaughter of Northern Dancer and half-sister to Chief's Crown, a winner of Saratoga's Travers Stakes. The auction block judgment on her prospects: $560,000.

Many of the heroes of August's opening week are four-legged: harnessed and prancing, they foray to the racetrack, polo field, and a challenging cycle of parties.

FOLLOWING PAGES
Perhaps the most unusual affair is the anything-goes dog show (p. 164, top) to benefit the Thoroughbred Retirement Farm at Walkill, New York. For Edna Morris as Popeye with Pluto, and Marylou Whitney, with Little Bo-Poodle, the Tuesday-afternoon affair at the track offers pleasant relief to more formal moments at the National Museum of Racing gala (p. 164, bottom) and the Travers Ball at the Hall of Springs (p. 165).

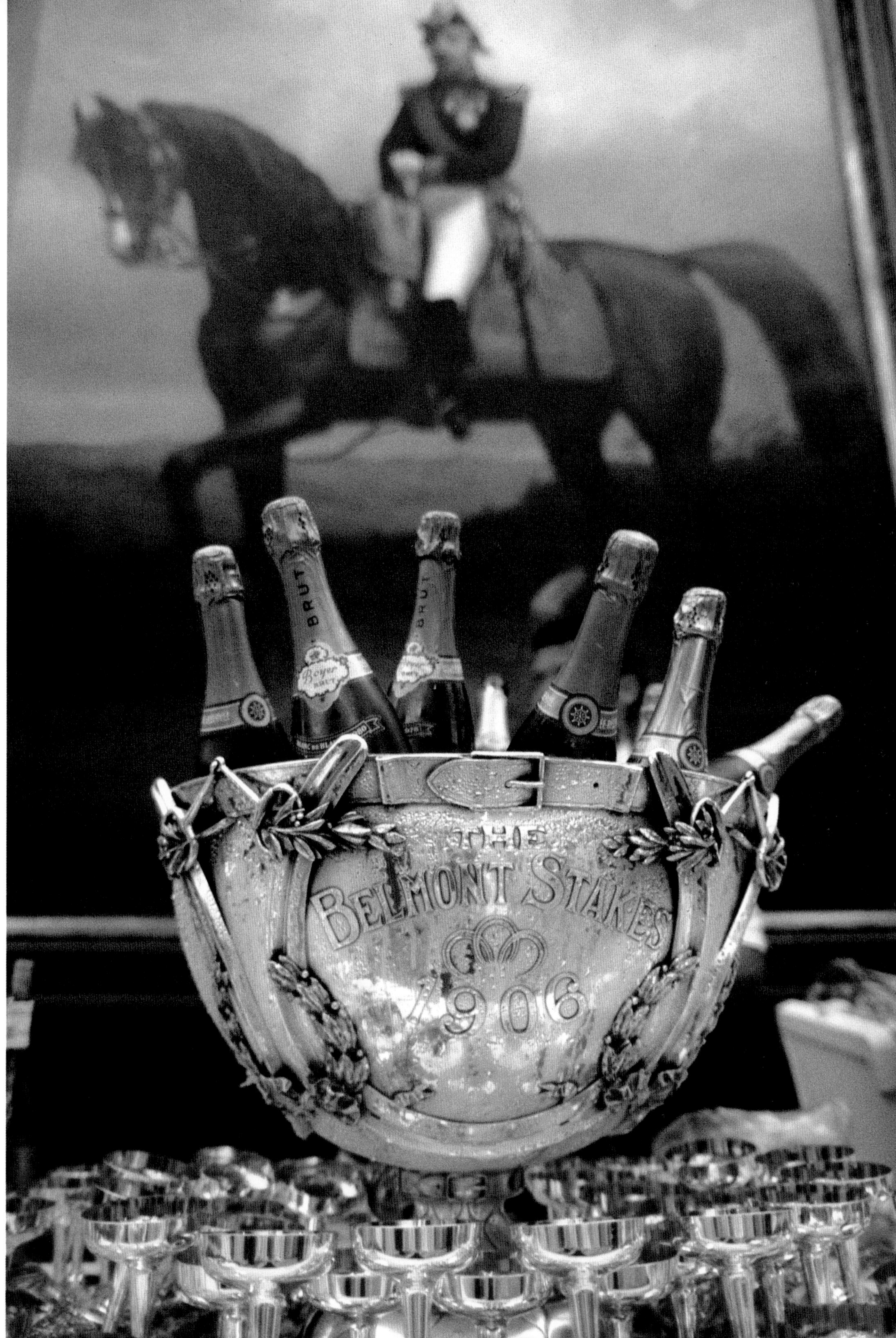
BRUT
BRUT
THE
BELMONT STAKES
1906

Today's Saratoga horseman, even if involved only peripherally in the racing industry, becomes duty bound to participate in a multitude of activities that can be described roughly as being done "for the good of the game." The phrase obviously has different meanings to horsemen, but common to most will be a calendar pockmarked with self-reminding memos that one or more—or all—of the following must be attended, or at least contemplated, during the meeting's first two weeks: National Steeplechase Day, three nights of Fasig-Tipton yearling sales, and meetings of The Jockey Club Research Foundation, The Jockey Club, The Jockey Club Round Table Conference, the Thoroughbred Racing Associations, the Breeders' Cup committees, the Thoroughbred Owners and Breeders Association, the Grayson Foundation, and the New York Thoroughbred Breeders.

Despite a few fancy and repetitious titles, much if not all of the business of these organizations centers around the conduct (including fund-raising chores) of various arms of the Thoroughbred racing industry. Annually included as topics for discussions are various aspects of equine research and veterinary medicine; issues of medication that vary from state to state; the uniformity of racing commission rules, which also vary from state to state; and, in general, matters pertaining to racing that appear to be in need of constant scrutiny or overhaul. The attendees are largely men and women with a sincere dedication to an unwritten law that says, if Thoroughbred racing is worth having at all, it should be both properly administrated and constantly improved.

Of a less serious nature, although beneficial in its way, is the mid-August Dog Show in the track paddock to benefit the Thoroughbred Retirement Foundation. Not to be confused with anything seen at the Westminster gathering in Madison Square Garden, this dog show gives prizes to every single entry, including the owner who most resembles his dog and the dainty three-year-old handler who can barely stagger around the required two or three laps of the walking ring.

Women, meanwhile, are having all they can handle sorting out the long and short rags that must be displayed somewhere come sundown. The list of somewheres is as exhausting as three miles over fences on soft turf. The Saratoga Hospital charity auction leads off the parade of events, traditionally held after the opening day of racing. Other charity or near-charity events have their moments, too. They include Empire State College's Evening with Lester Lanin, the Polo Luncheon to benefit Skidmore College, the dinner and entertainment at Yaddo, and most recently, the National Museum of Dance gala along with something along the lines of an Evening in Old Saratoga, which is highlighted by the appearance of assorted carriages and a mixed bag of drivers and their retinues.

There are also, naturally, functions related almost entirely to racing itself. Fasig-Tipton, the famous horse auction company, tosses a cocktail party at their sales ring a couple of nights before the three-night grind of sales gets under way. The National Museum of Racing puts on a ball in a tent erected just off the sidewalk of Union Avenue; the Travers Celebration (named after the classic race held on the third Saturday of the meeting)

OPPOSITE
Napoleon III, one of Saratoga's distinguished visitors, rides on at the Casino in Congress Park, where an heirloom punch bowl of Cornelius Vanderbilt Whitney's family harbors more recent arrivals from France. The occasion is Mrs. Whitney's private ball on the eve of the Whitney Stakes.

FOLLOWING PAGES
The rites of racing have been practiced at the Saratoga track since 1864; they are repeated nine times daily: the before-race buzz comparing choices (pp. 168–169); the starting bell, sending hope through the stands (pp. 170–171); and concern spreading through the crowd (pp. 172–173) as the horses head for the Clubhouse turn (pp. 174–175). There are urging hands (pp. 176–177) and flying turf (pp. 178–179); disappointment for some (pp. 180–181) and triumph for the likes of Angel Cordero aboard Chief's Crown in the 116th running of the Travers Stakes (pp. 182–183).

SARAT
UNITED
12
2B
11
1A
10
2
9

TOGA
8 7 6 5 1 4 3
UNITED

2
PERSIAN TIA

NEW YORK
SPALDING

10

1A

S

Many moments at Saratoga focus on triumph: the paddock strategy session, the last-minute betting choice, the groom's gear fence-sitting the race's outcome, the artist's pen enhancing the winning ticket.

FOLLOWING PAGES

And there is fine variety to racing on Saratoga's concentric ovals: the sandy-loam main course, the well-groomed turf, and the challenging steeplechase.

SARATOGA
THE SPINAWAY

DARK BAY
AUTOTOTE
THE BLOOD-HORSE of JULY 28, 1984

WIN PLACE SHOW
APPROXIMATE
STEEPLECH

ASE

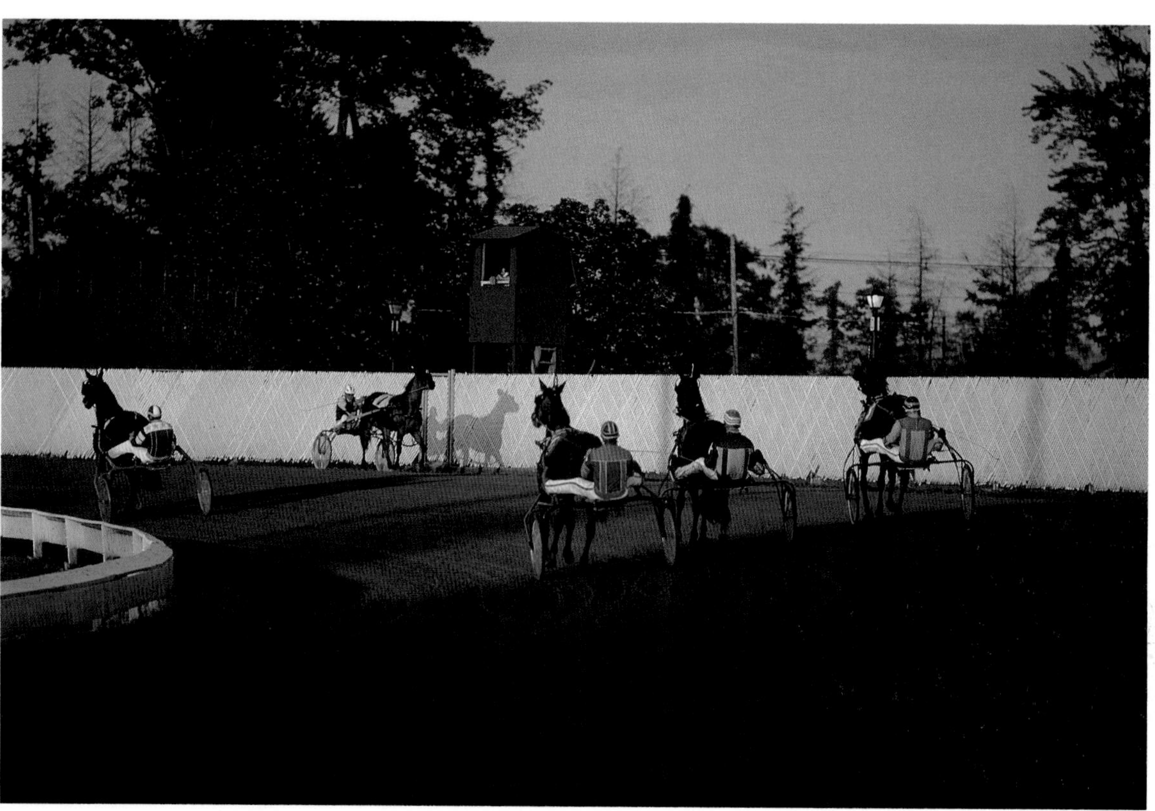

Day's end marks the beginning of an evening's harness racing at the Saratoga Raceway, which runs ten months a year.

dinner-dance gives everyone who hasn't already been there a shot at the Hall of Springs, which adjoins the theater of the Saratoga Performing Arts Center. And one cannot overlook the New York Turf Writers Association Awards Dinner—at which honors are bestowed on owners, breeders, trainers, and jockeys for top performances during the previous season. The pièce de résistance of all this is, of course, the C. V. and Marylou Whitney "do," which is very much a private "do," held on the first Friday, to be followed two nights later by the private dinner-dance given by Sue Whitmore at the Saratoga Golf and Polo Club.

The social and cultural rebirth that has taken place in Saratoga over the last decade or so has made the city overwhelmingly community conscious. Some citizens wearily total the number of summer charity functions already in existence—not to mention the charitable organizations that would be pleased to get so little as a toe in the doors opening to the sudden wealth of summer—and conclude that the addition of just one more benefit in August will be the straw that breaks the Thoroughbred's back.

The social functions already mentioned are more or less official, but of course, there are dozens of private luncheons, cocktail parties, and dinners that spring up daily, some launched quietly from the spacious porches of the North Broadway mansions, others slightly more elaborately. Any excuse for a party will do. Thus, Mary Sanford has traditionally given a birthday lunch for Mollie Wilmot, followed shortly by Mollie Wilmot's birthday dinner for Mary Sanford—neither is even on a birthday. The Sonny Werblins often toss a party in a private dining room at the Wishing Well, a popular local eatery, to

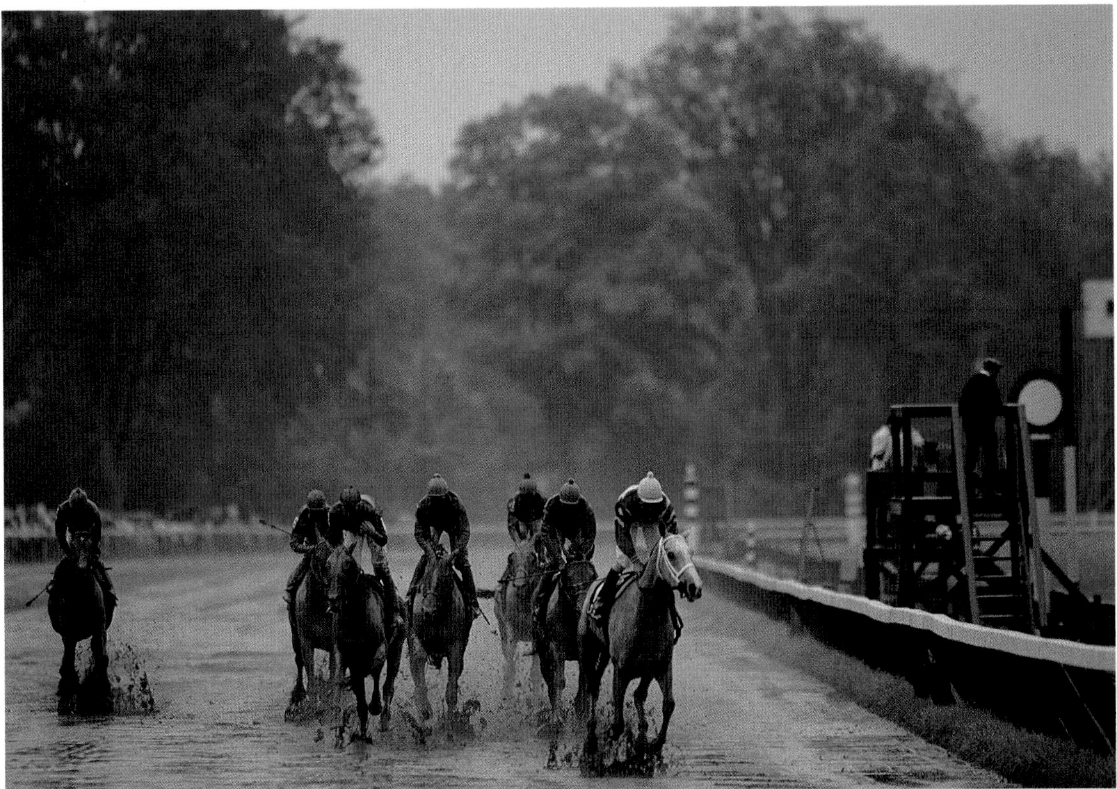

Leading "wire to wire," the filly Lady's Secret bears Eugene Klein's silks to pristine victory in the 1986 Whitney Stakes.

celebrate the wedding anniversary of the Ed McGraths. And trainer Woody Stephens sometimes gives a dinner for one hundred or so of his closest friends because, well, he's Woody Stephens, the only trainer in history ever to win five consecutive Belmont Stakes. Other trainers have stable parties at which the grooms, exercise boys, and the occasional jockey are the real guests of honor. Sometimes even the long-suffering, bill-paying owners are invited.

Jockeys in Saratoga, much like the men and women they ride for, have rarely been noted for their strict training habits. The incomparable Eddie Arcaro boasted openly that there was something about that clear, fresh air, not to mention that last 2 A.M. nightcap at Scotty's or King's—a couple of local gin mills heavily populated by stable personnel, the riding colony, and their friends—that seemed to provide him with a keener competitive edge the following afternoon. Arcaro always maintained he was at his best when under the most pressure, and Saratoga nights of four hours' sleep were capable of pumping up all the pressure anyone possibly could require.

There has always seemed to be a special camaraderie among all facets of the racing fraternity. There were exceptions, naturally, like the time when during a press-and-jockey softball game a volatile rider (now banished from racing) went after a writer with a baseball bat. He was repaying a compliment the reporter had paid him.

Jokes, pranks, and unforeseen accidents have been a part of the Saratoga scene since the beginning, along with parlor and dinner games. One might have foreseen, of course, casualties right, left, and all around during one recent dinner game when guests were asked to list the four women in

Rokeby Farm's owner Paul Mellon waits with jockey Jean-Luc Samyn for the call "riders up."

racing they would most like to avoid during the entire month of August. Considerably less character damage was achieved by two friends who rented houses across from one another one summer and spent much of their time away from the track spying on each other with binoculars to check out visitors. One evening, as Host A awaited the arrival of important clients for dinner, he noticed that Host B across the street was extending a welcoming hand to none other than George D. Widener, chairman of The Jockey Club. With a gleam of Irish wickedness in his eye, Host A hastily dispatched his butler to his friend's house carrying what the butler was to announce was a special pâté for so auspicious an occasion. Almost before the guests at Host B's house discovered that they had accepted a tasteless plate of Spam, Hostess B was revving up her car to dash to her racetrack stable. Within five minutes, a uniformed French waitress from B house was arriving at A house carrying a covered silver platter. Host A's guests could deduce from the smell, without lifting the cover, what sort of a surprise pâté *they* were being offered.

One house near the track was occupied three days each August by a crew of editors and writers from a national magazine. With nothing but gambling and good food and wine on their minds, this gang hit all the races at the flat track in the afternoon, dashed back to the house for a 6 P.M. dinner before heading off for the full harness program and then, from midnight until their wobbly frames could take it no longer, proceeded to engage in a high-stakes contest in which the objective was to roll a lemon toward—but not beyond—a certain mark on a carpet. Participating in such a Lemon-Off, as this game came to be known, was guaranteed to produce acute back problems if played after 4 A.M.

Almost as early as people began journeying to Saratoga in the Adirondack foothills to take the therapeutic waters, their interest has centered on horses. It has never waned, nor—and this may surprise some—has it always been centered exclusively on the Thoroughbred racing, as fine as that has been down through the years. Saratoga has a first-class Standardbred oval that consistently draws the best trotters and pacers in the eastern United States, and even if harness racing has always played second fiddle to the flat track in Saratoga, it does enjoy an annual long run and a steady nucleus of hard-core fans who turn out in all sorts of weather. Managed first by Ernest Morris and later by his son David, Saratoga Raceway has been part of the esteemed Grand Circuit of trotting and pacing since 1945. The nation's leading stables support Grand Circuit racing, and among the long-time stockholders and active participants in the sport at Saratoga were such familiar names as the Harry M. Stevens Company, one of the country's leading catering firms, and Dunbar Bostwick, whose brother Pete became a Hall of Fame steeplechase rider, and whose sister, the late Lillian Phipps, was the wife of former Jockey Club chairman Ogden Phipps. In April 1987 control of the track passed to what is now known as Saratoga Harness Racing, Inc. The immediate talk was of increased promotion and a larger colony of horses and drivers, but what does seem to be assured is the continuation of trotting at a track that has earned the respect of harness patrons and participants wherever Grand Circuit is conducted.

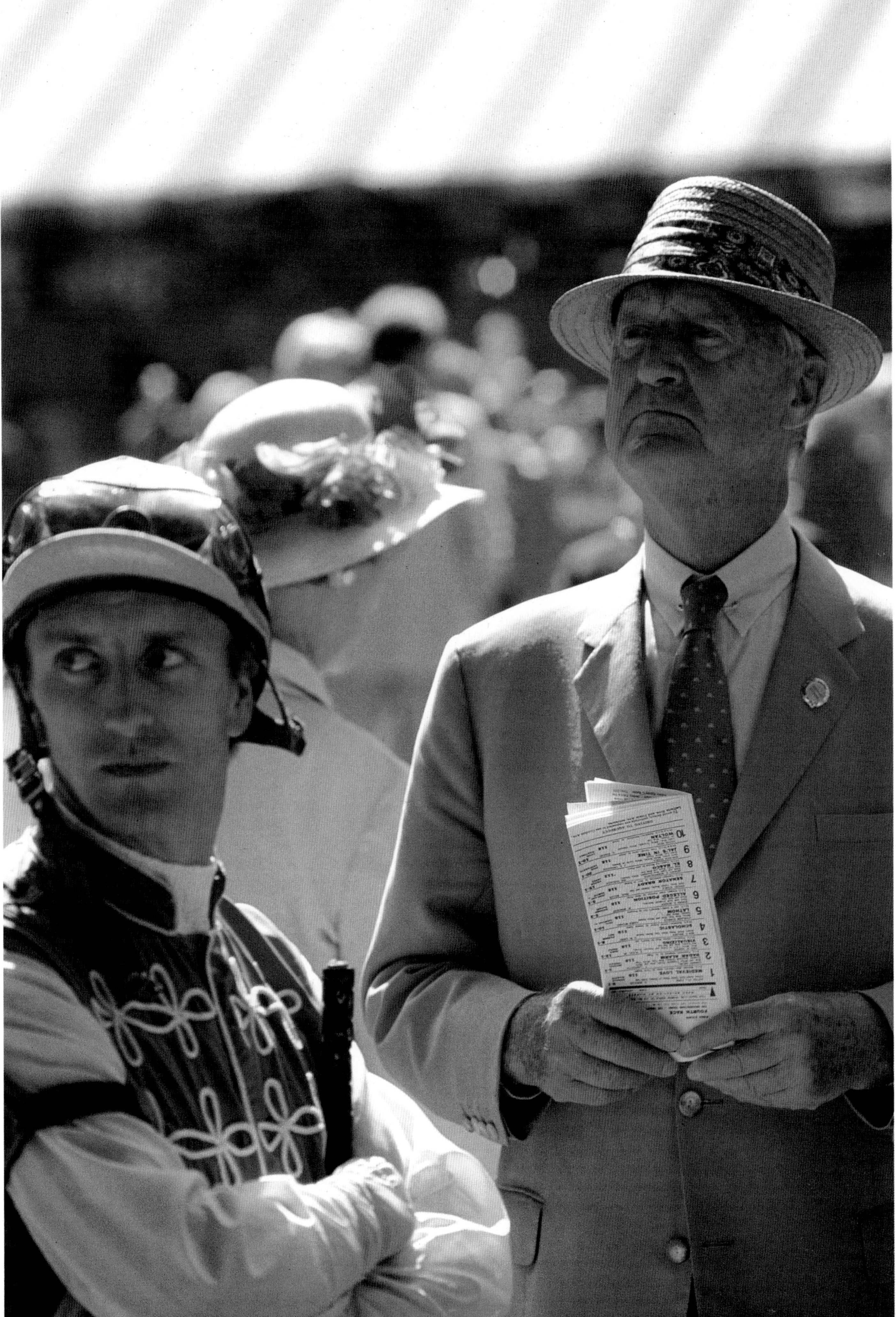
FOURTH RACE
1 MEDIEVAL LOVE
4 SCHOLASTIC
5 LATHOM
6 ALLEGED POSITION
7 SENATOR BRADY
10 WOLTAN

TEMPERENCE HILL
ANT COLONY
NICKLE, GUILTY CONSCIENCE

Many of the country's top steeplechasers and hurdlers are heard from during the season at the main track. The sport, which was once part of the scene at more than a dozen major tracks, has now largely been relegated to the country meetings where it all began—in places like Warrenton, Virginia, Nashville, Tennessee, Radnor, Pennsylvania, and Far Hills, New Jersey. But the NYRA still sees to it that a schedule of jump races is programmed at Saratoga—a few are still held at Belmont Park, too—but today these events chiefly serve as preps for the fall championships, which are usually decided in the Colonial Cup in Camden, South Carolina, and in the Breeders' Cup Steeplechase at Fair Hill, Maryland. The tradition of big-time 'chasing at major tracks lives mostly in the memories of surviving members of families with names like Clark, Hitchcock, duPont Scott, and Phipps-Bostwick.

With only 312 boxes in the Clubhouse and a 20-year waiting list, box holders doubly enjoy their finish-line vantage.

Polo reentered the Saratoga scene in the last decade, and some dozen or so of the country's top teams now show up for various tournaments. But the best players on the teams are Argentinians, who dominate the sport internationally, with a smattering of Mexican and British riders. Sponsored by American players or corporations (at over $100,000 a year), the recruits arrive with strings of Argentine-bred ponies, which are noted for their maneuverability and speed. Eventually, the ponies are sold and settle comfortably into stables in Palm Beach, Florida, Greenwich, Connecticut, and Oak Brook, Illinois, while their ex-owners depart with more bagsful of money—but that's another story.

Polo has become a spectator sport for many of the Saratoga locals chiefly because the sport presented to them is of the well-played, high-goal variety, and this is due in large part to the entrepreneurship of team-owning players like Will Farish and Peter Brant. Both men are prominent racehorse owners (Farish has twice been host to Queen Elizabeth II on her trips to Lexington, Kentucky), and they sponsor well-mounted teams, and Farish, at least, gives a polished respectability to the sport, which elevates it well above the level of the club polo seen in some other parts of the country. Brant, on the other hand, occasionally plays the role of the self-styled maverick, especially when, as a medium-handicapped player, he once saw fit to challenge the authority of the United States Polo Association. Threatened with disciplinary action for questioning the wisdom and the ruling of an on-field official, the hot-tempered Brant took steps to sue the sport's administrative body.

If there is anything wrong with the polo scene in Saratoga, it is only that it suffers from an overloaded social calendar. Except for Tuesdays, when there is no racing, the Thoroughbred crowd can rarely attend games, even when they are scheduled for 5 P.M. or later. For these people and others, polo directly competes with the golf courses, the baths, the sightseeing and shopping excursions, and if the truth be known, just plain sitting in a rocker on that old Saratoga porch and thinking about the next day's races or maybe next year's increased rent.

The main attraction, of course, is the annual twenty-four-day Thoroughbred race meeting, the very best short-term racing offered on this continent. It is a sort of quadrupled Royal Ascot Week in which the top horses are

Upset, W. Knapp up, beating Man O'War, J. Loftus, up
3rd Golden Broom, E. Ambrose, up "The Sanford" Saratoga, 1919
© C.C. COOK.

Man o' War's career had strong ties to Saratoga. As a yearling, he was sold here at auction. He returned to win five races and suffer his only loss. "Big Red" was among the first to be enshrined in the National Museum of Racing's Hall of Fame.

on display in a series of races that will, before year's end, help settle the question of several championships. Naturally, the horses are the leading three-year-old colts and fillies along with older campaigners of both sexes. And, there are also the two-year-olds, many still skittish and green but all of them hopeful.

It was not very long ago that Saratoga often *did* settle the championships. That it does not always do so these days can be attributed to new forces and trends affecting racing, some of them good, some not so good. On the plus side, I should think, is the Breeders' Cup, now in its fifth year. It was first proposed by John Gaines in order to attract national attention to racing and settle divisional championships in one fall afternoon swoop with a series of seven or eight races at a major track. The lure was $10 million in purse money. The thought was that no longer would the two-year-old who sparkled at Saratoga be a shoe-in for the Eclipse Award, emblematic of the best of his or her age, even, for example, if the horse followed with a victory in the Futurity at Belmont Park in September. Now, if the competition is anywhere close, the two-year-old is expected to meet its peers in a Breeders' Cup divisional race. The championship would be decided on the track, not at the ballot box.

The first Breeders' Cup series was run at Hollywood Park in 1984. Aqueduct had the honor the next year and Santa Anita in 1986. Hollywood Park got the races back in 1987. The reason for the geographical preference is TV. According to television and advertising people, it makes more sense to

Franklin D. Roosevelt's career included a few spins around Saratoga's track in 1931. He enjoyed the diversions of Governor's Day at the races while he served as New York state's chief executive.

begin a race card at 11 A.M. Pacific time (2 P.M. Eastern time) than it does to start racing at noon on the East Coast (when it would be 9 A.M. in the West) since there are more viewers. While the Breeders' Cup has done nothing to diminish the quality of racing at Saratoga, it has put on winners of Saratoga's classic stakes races the additional burden of having to do it all again in early November before the engraver has cut the name into the base of the Eclipse statuette. Considering the quality of Saratoga winners, this will not be an impossible assignment.

Tradition in racing is created at a pace well below that of the frisky Thoroughbred. In due time, the Breeders' Cup series will become a tradition, but not yet. Among New York stakes races, only three might be said to have earned instant status: the Woodward, first run in 1954; the now-discontinued Marlboro Cup, whose first running in 1973 was captured by Secretariat in world-record time; and the Turf Classic Stakes, inaugurated in 1977.

It is not just the ad man's attention to time zones that has advanced California's racing fortunes in recent years; progressive management and promotion have made California the legitimate rival of New York in providing the best year-round sport. In the same way that NYRA provides Easterners with a dependable, year-long circuit at Belmont, Aqueduct, and Saratoga, California gives Westerners Santa Anita, Hollywood Park, and in the summer, Del Mar, whose slogan is, "Where the Turf Meets the Surf"—and many consider it the Saratoga of the West. With a superior winter racing calendar that each year succeeds in attracting a handful of the top New York horses—

A photo-finish postcard was often used to send home news that a streak of luck was underway and the writer was extending his stay.

be it for the full season or merely for the major, and rich, stakes races—Santa Anita is superbly operated and the strongest reason why California shares racing's spotlight with New York.

All this is not an aside to the story of Saratoga, which, despite its short season, is very much part of the national racing scene. And what happens elsewhere has an effect here as well. Saratoga, for instance, has suffered the same bottom-line malaise, though fortunately to a lesser extent, that has infected all of American racing. Gone are the nonchalant pre-World War II days when all tracks were run by one man alone or by a group of friends and their carefully controlled companies. Generations of individual reigns at Saratoga, up through the late F. Skiddy von Stade in the early fifties, had treated racing as a sport first, business second. Sadly, now it is more often business first, sport nowhere. The nonprofit NYRA may have saved Saratoga and possibly Belmont and Aqueduct, but it sacrificed a vital side of the sport when it agreed to answer only to Albany, and Albany's quest—you might call it a never-ending howl—for more and more and more tax revenue.

Years ago, before Albany virtually demanded year-round racing in New York, Saratoga was for all practical purposes a championship season of itself. To be sure, a few titles became officially wrapped up in the fall at Belmont Park, but once we had done with the Futurity, the Beldame, the Jockey Club Gold Cup, and a few others there, tack and horses were packed up and the vans departed for the owners' farms in Maryland, Virginia, and Kentucky or, in later years, to one of the winter training quarters, perhaps

By 1941, the lucky postcard writer could be a "she." Only on the eve of World War II did the pari-mutuel system allow female bettors to step up to the window for themselves.

Aiken and Camden in South Carolina. Racing would not be scheduled again in New York until late March or April, which left plenty of time for all hands to attend either to business or, as often was the case, to reducing the duck and quail populations on plantations in the Carolinas, Georgia, or Florida.

Turn now to the present. We have Off Track Betting (OTB). In New York, the easiest way to bet the horses is to sit at home and use a telephone account to place your action. The next easiest is to drop around in person to one of the OTB shops, which, with few exceptions, possess all the warmth and charm of a detention cell. But you don't have to go to the track, and sometimes there is a sort of live action on the large-screen television.

Then how to account for what has been happening at Saratoga? There was a time when grandstanders came up from New York City in a caravan of buses that disgorged their passengers just before the daily-double windows closed. There are fewer buses today, yet in 1978 a Saratoga one-day record crowd of over 50,000 people showed up for the Travers Stakes featuring Affirmed vs. Alydar, which is about twice the year-round population of the town itself. Daily attendance has climbed in the last few years to over twenty-eight thousand, on average more people than there ever have been.

And the Clubhouse crowd, which might otherwise be occupied at Newport's Bailey's Beach or on the rock-bound coast of Maine, is in residence as before. The "elite," as they are sometimes called, arrive on the track grounds in a parade of Bentleys, Rollses, and other assorted town cars and limos and proceed in stately splendor to the Reading Room, the eating club

Famed Eddie Arcaro (second jockey from the left) led a field of Saratoga regulars raising funds for a World War II ambulance drive.

that is also convenient for parking. Just as well, since members can elect to use the distance to walk off the effects of the buffet line and its accompanying liquids. Unlike the grandstanders, they have not come to Saratoga necessarily to beat the horses. Many *own* horses, and they are not about to believe such chestnuts as the only way to get rich at the races is to pick up an unwanted gelding like John Henry for $1,500 and earn $6.5 million with him.

Owner-breeder Alfred Vanderbilt suggests that one logical reason why Saratogians and their summer visitors go racing is because everything is so nearby. The racetrack, he points out, is no more than five minutes by automobile from any area of town, which is surely better than the struggle one faces on New York's roads on the way to Belmont or Aqueduct. Many people walk to the Saratoga track from their rooms, others drive in for the day from Massachusetts, New Jersey, Vermont, or surrounding New York on highways that are relatively uncongested.

But primarily, it is racing itself that draws the crowds—and it is racing cast in the traditional mold, as it were, which is to say that the winners of Saratoga's four Saturday feature stakes, this year or next or ten years from now, are likely to go down in history with the great runners of the past, starting with the Whitney. The three wins each by Discovery (in the thirties) and Kelso (in the sixties) were outstanding achievements, but hardly more so than the 1986 victory by Lady's Secret, who became the first filly to beat males in the Whitney since Gallorette pulled off the feat in 1948. The most memorable Whitney was probably the shocker in 1973 when Triple Crown winner Secretariat was upset by Onion. Victorious trainer Allen Jerkens was so moved by what he had witnessed that he allowed himself a full-fledged cry as he walked to the winners' circle.

The second Saturday of the Saratoga meeting is given over to the Alabama Stakes, which ranks with the Coaching Club American Oaks as the most prestigious event for three-year-old fillies—and there never was a more popular win than Mom's Command in 1985. This was pretty much the sort of family affair to which Saratogians happily relate. Bostonian Peter Fuller, whose Dancer's Image had in 1968 suffered the only winner's disqualification in Kentucky Derby history, owned and bred Mom's Command. And for this Alabama, the chestnut granddaughter of Bold Ruler was brilliantly ridden to victory before a cheering Saratoga crowd by Fuller's daughter Abigail.

Known as the Mid-Summer Derby, the Travers Stakes for three-year-olds was first run in 1864 and was taken by a colt named Kentucky. This was eleven years before Aristides won the first Kentucky Derby. There have been many wonderful renewals of the Travers over the years; one certainly was the 1978 classic in which Alydar gained some measure of revenge for his three narrow Triple Crown losses to Affirmed by finally winning, albeit only after Affirmed had been disqualified.

As exciting, or more so, was the Travers of 1962. Jaipur, with Bill Shoemaker up, and Ridan, ridden by Manuel Ycaza, competed in a race that Hall of Fame trainer Max Hirsch claimed "The best horse race I ever saw." At the break in this mile-and-a-quarter test, both horses and both jockeys went at each other. They stayed together the full distance, stride for stride, and at the finish, as thousands cheered, only the camera could certify that Belmont Stakes winner Jaipur had triumphed by a nose. Both colts covered themselves with lasting glory that brilliant afternoon.

Saratoga's final weekend features the Hopeful for two-year-old colts. As the name implies, the leading finishers are the colts one expects to hear much more from in the three-year-old classics the following season, and the Hopeful repeatedly has lived up to the wish. It has signaled the timely arrival of, among others, Man o' War, Native Dancer, Nashua, and Buckpasser, along with such Triple Crown horses as Whirlaway, Secretariat, and Affirmed.

Saratoga has not been without its problems. At one juncture, some of the pari-mutuel clerks went on strike; at another, immigration officials came around and successfully sniffed out fourteen illegal aliens; and to the dismay of thousands, the Saratoga stewards once found themselves guilty of disqualifying the wrong horse—when the "OFFICIAL" light blinked on, there was not much the outraged losing betters could do except, maybe, recall the occasion several years before when racing's leading starter, George Cassidy, sent a field away on what he considered another perfect start only to discover that the outside horse really was outside—outside the gate, that is, partially hidden by his lead pony.

Healthy—booming, some people say—Saratoga racing appears to be in no danger. In fact, one of the rosier signs for the future is the growing number of breeding farms and training establishments springing up through-

THIS PAGE
Louis Giscard d'Estaing presents the Dom Ruinart Cup to Alan Connell for the Las Cachinas polo team's victory over Saratoga.
OPPOSITE
The Tailgate Picnic Contest at the Saratoga Polo Fields is judged by Frances Ingraham, Marylou Whitney, and Whitney Tower. The winning entry gets eaten—with extra bottles of the finest champagne.

out the state. Fully in tune with this local development, the NYRA schedules an increasing number of races, including several major stakes, restricted to New York breds. State-provided bonuses for owners who win these restricted races should make for sterner competition as the program matures. New York also is slowly acquiring some of the better stallions that in former times would have been hustled off to Kentucky, Florida, California, Maryland, or Virginia.

The sole cloud on Saratoga's horizon, one that causes horsemen to pull on their long, gloomy faces, is the occasional downward direction taken in the yearling sales ring. Conducted by Fasig-Tipton, the Saratoga sales have ranked traditionally second in volume only to the summer sales at Keeneland, and both have been noticeably off from the high-flying days when the best stock usually was snapped up by high-bidding Robert Sangster, the British bookmaker, or Sheikh Mohammed bin Rashid al-Maktoum and his fellow princes from the Persian Gulf emirate of Dubai. Admitting that, with prices twenty-seven percent off, many yearlings in the 1986 market did not bring enough to cover the stud fees that produced them, Fasig-Tipton president John Finney told *Fortune Magazine*, "You can kiss the limited partnership goodbye." In the same article, Sangster's chief buying agent, Irishman Tom Cooper, dipped into his fedora and pulled out the old and trusted truism of which any Saratoga regular would approve, "We should never forget that this sport is built on two four-letter words—hope and luck." The luck turned in 1987 as averages suddenly climbed over twenty percent.

It has been that way around the Saratoga track since 1863. No reason to think it will be any different for the next one hundred twenty-five years.

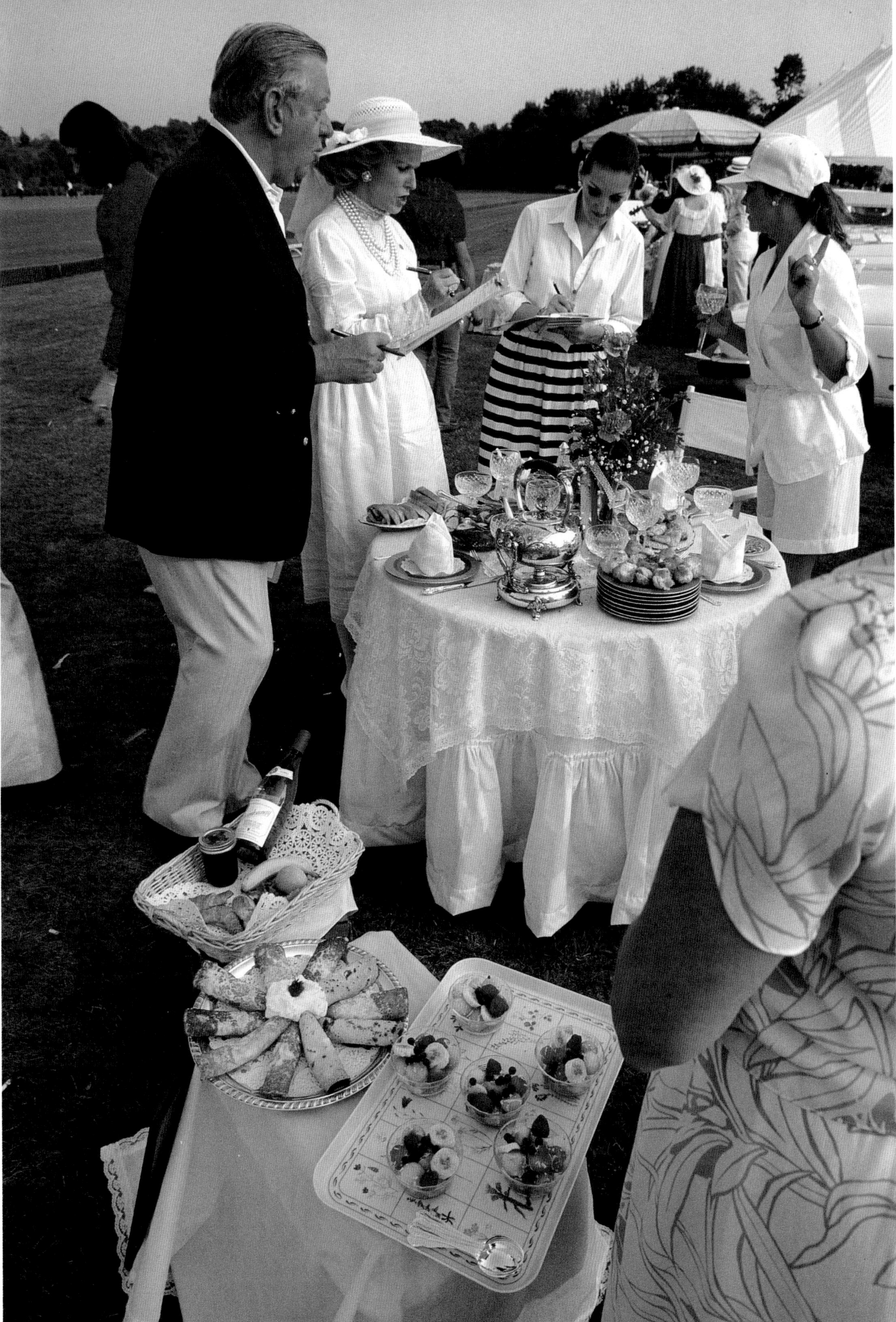

"To the Mallet Born": Children of the polo world enjoy a joust on the sidelines while a slightly older generation bids adieu before taking to the field. The August card of seventeen matches between five teams continues a summer's high-goal polo competition, which begins at Greenwich, Connecticut, in June. Top players from North and South America—both professional and amateur—offer Saratoga visitors astonishing equestrian skill and daring.

OPPOSITE AND FOLLOWING PAGES
When White Birch and Centennial Farms clash (pp. 203–205), each of the eight players has a string of fresh ponies—at least six—to carry them through six furious chukkers of polo. Victor and vanquished (pp. 206–207) know that at day's end in Saratoga, night is only beginning, and at season's end, the next season is on its way.

CF

3
WHITE BIRCH

3
1
2